D0742017

CALGARY PUBLIC LIBRARY

SEP   2017

EAT LIKE A
ROCK STAR

MORE THAN 100 RECIPES FROM ROCK & ROLL'S GREATEST

MARK BEGO

INTRODUCTION BY MARY WILSON OF THE SUPREMES

Skyhorse Publishing

Copyright © 2017 by Mark Bego

All rights reserved. No part of this book may be reproduced in any manner without the express written consent of the publisher, except in the case of brief excerpts in critical reviews or articles. All inquiries should be addressed to Skyhorse Publishing, 307 West 36th Street, 11th Floor, New York, NY 10018.

Skyhorse Publishing books may be purchased in bulk at special discounts for sales promotion, corporate gifts, fund-raising, or educational purposes. Special editions can also be created to specifications. For details, contact the Special Sales Department, Skyhorse Publishing, 307 West 36th Street, 11th Floor, New York, NY 10018 or info@skyhorsepublishing.com.

Skyhorse® and Skyhorse Publishing® are registered trademarks of Skyhorse Publishing, Inc.®, a Delaware corporation.

Visit our website at www.skyhorsepublishing.com.

10 9 8 7 6 5 4 3 2 1

Library of Congress Cataloging-in-Publication Data is available on file.

Cover design by Jenny Zemanek
Cover photo credit by Mark Bego
Photographs by Mark Bego

Print ISBN: 978-1-5107-2115-9
Ebook ISBN: 978-1-5107-2119-7

Printed in China

Dedication

In loving memory to three dear friends: Jimmy Greenspoon of Three Dog Night, Barbara Shelley, and Don Kevern. All three of these people, each in different ways, greatly influenced my life and my writing career. To this trio, I lovingly dedicate this book.

Jimmy Greenspoon devoted his life to the rock group Three Dog Night and his vast circle of family and friends. I was honored to be one of his friends, having cowritten his autobiography, *One Is the Loneliest Number.* When I told him about *Eat Like a Rock Star* he was so excited he not only gave me a pair of his favorite recipes but, with his boundless enthusiasm, would also phone me every couple of weeks to ask when we were going on TV together to cook and promote the book. When he passed away in 2015, he left behind a wealth of music that will be his legacy.

Barbara Shelley was a music industry publicist extraordinaire, and one of my dearest friends. She was a champion of my writing career from the minute she met me in 1975 to the last days of her life. We went to parties and openings, danced at Studio 54, and had forty years of fun together. She introduced me to her many clients, including Aretha Franklin, Micky Dolenz, and Cher, all three of whom became the subjects of hugely successful music biographies that were written by me. We had lots of rock & roll adventures together, and she absolutely loved the idea of the book that you are now holding in your hands.

Don Kevern was one of my junior high school English teachers. He was so proud of me when I hit the *New York Times* best seller list–not once, but twice. Don was especially thrilled that one of his students–me!–had taken what I learned from his teachings and accomplished such an achievement. He was a dear friend who always encouraged me and my writing career throughout the years.

TABLE of CONTENTS

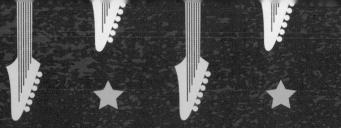

Acknowledgments

Cindy Adams, J. J. Arévalo, Paul Antonelli, Bobby Bank, Kathy Bego, Mary and Bob Bego, Angela Bowie, Rudy Calvo, Freddy Cannon, Debby Campbell, Jay Cassell, Lou Christie, Rita Coolidge, Tom Cuddy, Donnie Dacus, August Darnell aka Kid Creole, Sarah Dash, Billy Davis, Jr., Cory Daye, Dennis DeYoung, Donna Dolenz, Micky Dolenz, Alyse Dorese, Gregory Eddings, Walter Egan, Joey Fatone, Duncan Faure, Pete Filleul, Nicole Frail, Abigail Gehring, Debbie Gibson, Susaye Greene, Jimmy Greenspoon, Barbara Halterman, Jim Halterman, David Hanshaw, Balázs Havasi, Thelma Houston, Tommy James, Randy Jones, Sergio Kardenas, Betty Kelly, Alan LaFever, Anne LaFever, Heather LaFever, Michelle LaFever, Sean Lennon, Kim Lim, Alice Lizee, Marcy MacDonald, Dave Marken, Marilyn McCoo, Melanie, Michael McDonald, Spanky McFarlane, Kevin Milburn, Larry Nicola, Terri Nunn, Ray Parker, Jr., Elaine Parker, Freda Payne, Scherrie Payne, Michelle Phillips, Al Pontillo, Martha Reeves, Carol Ross, David Salidor, Richie Sambora, Boz Scaggs, "Chef" Benny Schneider, Jay Siegel, Barbara Shelley, Andy Skurow, Jade Starling, Shawn Stockman, Derek Storm, Tiffany, Tanya Tucker, Katherine Turman, Cherry Vanilla, George Vissichelli, Beth Wernick, Mari Wilson, Mary Wilson, Bill Wyman

Special thanks to Mary Wilson, David Hanshaw, and Dave Marken:

Mary Wilson, you believed in this project from the very beginning. First of all, your recipes are fantastic, and they literally are responsible for inspiring this entire book. Thank you so much for helping me reach out to so many of my guest chefs included in this book, and for forty years of dear friendship. You are truly Supreme!

David Hanshaw, you were very supportive of my crazy photo sessions featuring the food that is in this book. You acted as my stylist, my critic, and my sounding board. Then when it came time to promote this book, you helped with my television food demonstrations and whatever other crazy schemes I came up with along the way.

Dave Marken, my amazing manager! You loved the idea of this book from the moment I mentioned it to you in 2013. You helped me set up the blog that gave birth to this book, you got me auditions at The Food Network, and no matter what anyone else said, you stuck with me until this book became a reality. You rock, Marken!

Introduction
BY MARY WILSON

I have known Mark Bego since 1975 when he first interviewed me for an article in *Record World* magazine. From our first meeting, we became instant lifelong best friends, and since that time we have traveled all over the world together. Mark helped me write both of my best-selling autobiographies, *Dreamgirl: My Life as a Supreme* and *Supreme Faith: Someday We'll Be Together*. He has also spotlighted quotes from me in several of his sixty-two published books. In addition, he has hosted my birthday parties, babysat my children, and on one particular tour of Japan and Korea even served as my road manager and stage manager. We have gambled and won money together at the Kentucky Derby; we have gone to Monaco to dance all night with Prince Albert; and we've been in Sweden together partying with the always gracious Princess Christina. We have collaborated on so many projects that we could write a book about our many shared adventures. And, amidst it all, we have had some incredible food together!

In Japan, while my band members were going to the local branches of American fast food chains, Mark and I were eating at all of the yakitori restaurants we could find: from Okinawa to Misawa. We have had pastries together in Paris, amazing Italian food in Louisville, sushi in Tokyo, and fresh seafood in Monte Carlo. And, it

Credit: MJB Photo Archives

Longtime friends Mark Bego and Mary Wilson in 2017, on their way to celebrate The Academy Awards Night Gala, Night of 100 Stars, in Los Angeles, California.

isn't just fine cuisine that we appreciate together; we have also eaten currywurst in Germany, ramen in Los Angeles, deli sandwiches in New York City, and even fabulous hot dogs after midnight from street vendors in Stockholm.

Mark Bego and I have also cooked some great food for each other. He still reminds me of a seafood soup, which I made for him in his Greenwich Village apartment, and my beet soup, prepared at his house in Tucson. He came out to Las Vegas one March, and he and my daughter, Turkessa, spent all day making hors d'oeuvres for my birthday party.

I loved the idea of this cookbook from the moment he mentioned it to me. Mark has not only gathered recipes from our rock star friends, but he has also proved that he can cook as well, and every chapter of this book contains some of his favorite recipes.

I truly believe that cooking and sharing food for your family and your friends is one of the most personal gifts you can give them. That is what this book is all about, and this is why I am so happy to be a part of it. We all share parts of our lives and our experiences by cooking for one another. This isn't just a colorful cookbook that you are holding in your hands; it is the product of years of culinary experiences by some of the most talented and gifted celebrities in the rock & roll world. Every rock star in this book has personally shared their favorite recipes with Mark, and through these pages they, in turn, share them with you. I am glad to be one of them.

Where else can you have chicken with Boz Scaggs, pasta with Michael McDonald, soul food with Martha Reeves, Polynesian chicken with Marilyn McCoo, appetizers with Joey Fatone, lamb with Bill Wyman of The Rolling Stones, a cocktail with Micky Dolenz of The Monkees, gumbo with Freda Payne, and dessert with Tanya Tucker?

This is the book that will show you how you can do exactly that.

I am officially inviting you to come along on an incredible food journey with Mark and me and dozens of our rock & roll friends. We are about to show you how you, too, can truly *Eat Like a Rock Star*!

Credit: Cherie Smith

Colorfully clad for the 2015 Kentucky Derby, Mary Wilson and Mark Bego are "Red Carpet ready" for the cameras.

"Touch"
MARY WILSON

Mary

Preface

Welcome to my dream cookbook, *Eat Like a Rock Star*. I am Mark Bego, the author of sixty-two books on rock & roll and show business, with over twelve million copies in print and two *New York Times* best sellers. I have written books on Madonna, Michael Jackson, Cher, Whitney Houston, Bette Midler, Elton John, Billy Joel, The Doobie Brothers, Barry Manilow, Tina Turner, Joni Mitchell, Aretha Franklin, Bonnie Raitt, Jackson Browne, Martha Reeves & The Vandellas, The Village People, The Monkees, and many more. You must be asking yourself, "So how is it that this guy is suddenly an expert on food and writing his own cookbook?" Well, here is my story.

I was writing and working with Mary Wilson on a "special edition" magazine entitled *My Supremes: A 50th Anniversary Celebration* in 2012. While highlighting Mary's glamorous career with The Supremes, I got an idea that it should also feature two pages of Mary's recipes. After the magazine was published and became a big hit, I found that the recipe pages were one of my favorite parts of the magazine.

My imagination began to wander. *What if I came up with a whole book of rock & roll celebrities and their food? I wonder if anyone would be aboard for this? Because I think I am onto something big!*

After having interviewed so many rock stars over the years, I was still in contact with many of them, which would certainly help to get the ball rolling. My close, longtime friend, Mary Wilson, agreed to let me use her recipes from the magazine as a starting point.

"Would other rock stars give me recipes as well?" I asked myself. My first test was Boz Scaggs. We had an upcoming interview for a feature story I was writing about him and his 2013 album, *Memphis*.

Credit: Charles Moniz

Mary Wilson and I have been best friends since I first interviewed her in 1975. Here we are at the Manhattan nightclub New York, New York, in August of 1979 for her solo debut when she disbanded The Supremes.

LEFT: If ever there was a dream project for me to work on, it is this cookbook! I have had so much fun cooking, writing, and photographing all of the food photos on these pages. It has connected and reconnected me with so many incredible rock stars as well. Credit: Sergio Kardenas

Since I found out that he had his own line of wine for sale, it seemed like a natural conclusion that he could cook, too.

After interviewing him about his music, I told him that I was planning a rock & roll cookbook and wondered aloud if he had a recipe for me. Much to my surprise and delight, he did! A few days later, I found three variations on chicken recipes from Boz Scaggs himself in my email inbox.

Then it became a matter of "rounding up the usual suspects"! The next person I called was Jimmy Greenspoon, keyboard player for Three Dog Night. Jimmy and I had been dear friends since we wrote his memoir *One Is the Loneliest Number* (1991). I said to him, "You must have a recipe for chili: Three Alarm Chili! Can't you see it? Three Dog Night Three Alarm Chili!" The next thing I knew, I had that recipe from him, along with his signature spaghetti sauce.

Randy Jones, the original cowboy from The Village People, has been one of my best friends since we met in the 1970s. Randy and I also wrote a book together called *Macho Man* (2009). During one of his recent visits to my house, we made an excellent batch of minestrone soup together. I had another rock star recipe.

I was speaking to my dear friend Marcy MacDonald, and I told her about my cookbook idea. She immediately said, "Well, you should call Michelle Phillips. Here, I will give her your number and tell her to expect your call." Soon, I was on the phone with the legendary willowy, blonde star of The Mamas & The Papas, one of my first favorite rock groups. She insisted that I try her recipe for Organic Lemon Chicken. I tried it, I loved it, and here it is on these pages—and is it ever delicious! You will find yourself vividly "California Dreamin." . . .

Then something crucial happened. My manager, Dave Marken said to me, "Okay, you have the beginnings of a cookbook here. But how are people going to seek you out as a cook and a food expert? You have to prove that you can cook too. Why don't I set up a website for you, and let's start posting recipes you come up with, as well as the celebrity recipes? That will help launch the cookbook."
"That's the ticket!" I instantly said in agreement.

The beginnings were now in place. With the advice of my manager, Dave Marken, I started the blog *Cook Like a Rock Star* in November 2013, to document my culinary journey. I began with a couple of recipes I had been making for years, such as Cold Spicy Szechuan Sesame Noodles, Rigatoni Bolognese, and Boozy Banana Cream Pie. I also experimented with more challenging recipes, such as making Green Tea Macarons with Buttercream Frosting with my niece, Heather LaFever, and coming up with my own twist on a scone to perfect my famous Cherry Pineapple Almond Scones.

I advertised the blog on Facebook and Twitter, and suddenly people started to respond—by the thousands. The next thing I knew, dear friend Cindy Adams, gossip columnist extraordinaire, wrote

Credit: Simon Lazer

When I got into the whole cookbook frame of mind, for Halloween I decided to channel my childhood cooking hero, Chef Boyardee.

about it in her *New York Post* column: "Author Mark Bego, whose Omnibus book on Glen Campbell's out in April, got a food blog. Recipes from The Mamas & Papas' Michelle Phillips, Mary Wilson of The Supremes, Boz Scaggs. Obviously, nonsingers don't eat!" I also auditioned as a contestant on the popular Food Network program *Chopped*.

Next came the push to find more rock star recipes. I have known Angela Bowie, another of my best friends, since the 1970s. Though she first became famous while married to David Bowie, she has blossomed into a successful author and recording artist, and she sure knows her way around a kitchen! When she lived in Tucson, we were known for our lunches together, when we would spend a lot of time talking about and sampling each other's cooking. She gladly shared a couple of her favorite recipes with me for this book, such as her famed Cowboy Cookies.

Cherry Vanilla, another longtime friend who is also from the Bowie camp, provided her incredible "Quick and Stiff" Spinach Lasagna recipe.

My "dirty martini" buddy, Paul Antonelli from the eighties group Animotion, shared his favorite salmon recipe, as well as a cocktail to go with it!

Michael McDonald of The Doobie Brothers, whom I have known since 1976 when I interviewed him and Patrick Simmons for *Good Times* magazine, is always so warm and wonderful whenever I run into him. He and I were, coincidentally, on the same flight together from Nashville to Los Angeles in 2014. When we got off the plane, he gave me his recipe for Pasta with Ham, Peas, and Parmesan Cheese while we were in the baggage claim area of LAX.

Credit: Bobby Bank

I moved to New York City from Michigan in 1974, diving into my career as a rock & roll journalist. When I interviewed Patrick Simmons (left) and Michael McDonald (right) at the St. Regis Hotel in 1976, I had no idea that Michael would one day be part of my first celebrity cookbook!

I have known Micky Dolenz of The Monkees since we wrote his memoir, *I'm a Believer*, in 1993. He shares one of his favorite cocktail recipes here, The Micky "D."

I have known Debbie Gibson since she was sixteen years old, when I was a rock music writer in New York City. Together, we wrote the book *Between the Lines* (1989) about her life and her career, my first celebrity collaboration biography. Her vegan Coconut Biscuits are absolutely delicious!

Another great source of recipes has been through the Kentucky Derby, which I have attended on several occasions with my favorite collaborator and best friend, Mary Wilson. As guests at the annual Barnstable Brown Gala in Louisville, Kentucky, we became friendly with other regular attendees, such as Joey Fatone of 'N Sync, Shawn Stockman of Boyz II Men, Tanya Tucker, and Marilyn McCoo and Billy Davis Jr.

Joey Fatone has got to be one of the friendliest, nicest, and most fun guys in show business. Not only does he act and sing, but he also likes to cook and has appeared on several TV shows on the Food Network—including hosting his own cooking competition, *Rewrapped*. Joey's Rice Balls, which appear in this book, are excellent.

Shawn Stockman of Boyz II Men is an incredibly nice guy, as well. We met while we were standing in line to place bets at Churchill Downs—he was in front of me. I found out that two of his favorite dishes are Asian Fusion Garlic Noodles and Ginger Red Sea Bass, which, thanks to Shawn, you will find here.

While I originally met Tanya Tucker in the 1970s, we were reacquainted in 2016 when Mary Wilson and I were at The Kentucky Derby. My friend Beth Wernick was Tanya's publicist when her totally rock & roll album *T-N-T* came out back in 1978. (I will never forget the party in Tanya's honor at One Fifth in New York City to celebrate the album's release.) Here, Tanya shares two of her favorite recipes with me: Chicken Mole Enchilada Casserole and Chocolate Chip Peanut Butter Chip Cookies.

I met the wonderful and charming Marilyn McCoo and Billy Davis Jr. of The Fifth Dimension in 1977 when I interviewed them for an article in *Us Magazine*. Not only do they harmonize beautifully together, but they can both cook, too. After running into Marilyn at Churchill Downs at the Kentucky Derby, she told me about four of her favorite recipes: Dr. Mary's Grits Casserole, marinated Leg of Lamb, Aunt Mil's Polynesian Chicken, and Sheila's Dressing. I immediately knew I had hit the jackpot!

Martha Reeves, the incredible hit-making star, wrote her best-selling 1994 memoir, *Dancing in the Street: Confessions of a Motown Diva*, with me as co-author. She visited and stayed at my house in Tucson while I was writing the book, and she demonstrated her cooking skills several times. I will never forget sitting at my dining room table to edit the latest chapter, when I looked up to see her cooking in my kitchen and singing to The Beatles' *Magical Mystery Tour* album. I thought I had died and gone to Motown heaven! Here, Martha shares her true soul food mastery with Smoked Turkey Necks & Lima Beans recipe.

The same thing happened with Sarah Dash, of the sizzling singing trio LaBelle. When she visited me in Tucson, we took turns cooking for each other. She told me incredible stories of her singing partners Patti LaBelle and Nona Hendryx, and what Keith Richards of The Rolling Stones was like to tour with. Let me tell you: Sarah Dash can really cook, especially with her recipes Spinach Sauté and Sugar Cookie Peach Cobbler!

In the 1970s, I met folk rock singer Melanie when I interviewed her and her record producer husband, Peter Schekeryk, for an article in *Us Magazine*. In the 1990s, Melitta Coffee launched a line of special celebrity coffees, and since I was on *The New York Times* best-seller list at the time with my book *Leonardo DiCaprio:*

Romantic Hero, and because of Peter's association with Melitta at the time, I had my very own "Mark Bego Romantic Hero Blend" of hazelnut coffee! (I still have several packages of the coffee in my house.) Here, you will find Cheesy Corn on the Cob, one of Melanie's favorites.

I was in Nashville with Debby Campbell in September of 2014 to promote our book on her father, Glen Campbell, when she gave me her favorite recipe for Mexican Tortilla Chicken Casserole, which she used to whip up for her dad.

While on that same trip to Nashville, I had coffee with Tiffany at a charming café, not far from her one-of-a-kind antique clothing boutique: Tiffany's Boutique. She was absolutely lovely, and we had a great conversation about her music, her store, her career, and her love of cooking. I was thrilled when she gave me her wonderful recipe for Lebanese Cinnamon Chicken, which is incredibly delicious!

Credit: Derek Storm

In my mind, there is nothing like pasta! The recipes you can cook up using pasta are absolutely endless. Here I am in Greenwich Village, getting into a plate of linguini.

Bill Wyman of The Rolling Stones is someone I'm really happy to have met. We were first acquainted in Monaco in 2008 and we got to know each other better during a pan-European rock & roll bus tour with Bill Wyman's Rhythm Kings, featuring Mary Wilson as the special guest star. On our way to Copenhagen, I asked Bill for a recipe. He jokingly said, "The only thing I make is a cup of Earl Grey tea."

I replied, "Really, Bill? You must cook something."

He thought for a moment and said, "Well, I do make lamb chops and an incredible endive salad."

That was all I needed as a lead-in. Five minutes later I had the whole recipe on paper, Lamb Chops with Endive Salad, right down to the bleu cheese crumbles for the accompanying endive salad!

Now, a little bit about my own cooking experiences.

With rare exception, I am self-taught in the art of cooking. As a teenager, I recall being at home and asking my mother if she would bake a cake. She said, "There's the kitchen; there's the cookbook. It's about time you learned to bake your own cake."

So, I did! I loved to experiment, too. My entire family recalls the cake I made, with blue wintergreen-flavored frosting. The cake—made from scratch—came out perfectly. However, there is a reason you never see a white cake with wintergreen frosting: it tastes like toothpaste!

My first job during high school was as the cashier and French fry maker at the local Burger Chef in Pontiac, Michigan. In college at Central Michigan University, my first part-time job was working for Johnny Giovanni at Giovanni's pizza. He was the one who taught me how to make a great pizza crust. After we baked several pizzas, I would drive them to a local college bar where I sold them by the slice from table to table. One summer, I worked as a short order cook at Howard Johnson's at Maple and Telegraph in Bloomfield Hills, Michigan, very quickly learning to make eggs, hash brown potatoes, and hamburgers—as well as Howard Johnson's trademark deep-fried clams—to-order. During college, I was also a wiz at making spaghetti sauce out of just about anything—even ketchup—that could be found in the little apartment I lived in with three other roommates. Especially if we were coming home at two in the morning after partying at the local bars, I would be in the kitchen making ketchup tomato sauce!

Credit: David Salidor

In 2010, I hosted a party at my favorite Italian restaurant in Manhattan, Aleo, on West 21st Street. Here I am with three of my biography co-authors, who are now three of my co-chefs in this book: Randy Jones of The Village People, Micky Dolenz of The Monkees, and Debbie Gibson.

After I graduated with a degree in broadcasting, film and theater, and journalism, I moved to New York City and quickly learned how to cook in a tiny Greenwich Village apartment, including how to throw dinner parties on a budget. It was in the

1970s that I first became friends, and later best buddies, with Mary Wilson of The Supremes. She would stay with me at my apartment in the 1980s, which is when we started cooking together. I distinctly remember Mary making a great seafood soup in my miniature kitchen on East 11th Street. On a Saturday night in 1976, Cory Daye and August Darnell (aka Kid Creole), as well as the entire Dr. Buzzard's Original Savannah Band, stopped over at my little Greenwich Village apartment prior to their midnight performance at 12 West. We were all so "financially compromised" at that time that I served cherry Kool-Aid and cheap vodka for cocktails. Ah, the Disco Era! This book has helped me reconnect with both of them, and their recipes are also on these pages–Empanadas, Seven People Salmon, and Lilikoi Lemon Drop.

Credit: Kévin J. Ziane

My lifelong passion for good food has helped as an inspiration for this book. Here I am in Paris, immersing myself in the culture–and the food!

I have come a long way from those days in Greenwich Village. As time has gone by, I have stepped up my kitchen game and added more and more things to my recipe repertoire, challenging myself to really cook an eclectic list of dishes, from French macarons and donuts to Chinese stir-fry and cabbage rolls.

I spoke to publishers for two years about my idea for a cookbook full of rock stars. In the fall of 2015, I was invited to lunch by my editor and friend, Jay Cassell, at Skyhorse Publishing, who recently published my books *Aretha Franklin: The Queen of Soul* (2012) and *Whitney Houston!* (2012). Along with cookbook editor Nicole Frail, we hammered out Skyhorse's concept for the cookbook. I signed my publication contract in the summer of 2016, began work with Skyhorse editor Kim Lim, and here we are!

What I present in *Eat Like a Rock Star* features not only the most fun and exciting potpourri of rock star recipes possible—you will also get three or more of my own culinary creations per chapter, which I hope will stretch this book into new culinary directions.

Since I am best known as a rock & roll biographer, this book also includes mini biographies of all my rock star celebrity chefs. You may be inspired not only to cook their recipes, but also to go out and buy their vinyl records and CDs or download their albums.

The recipes you will find in this book were not clipped out of magazine articles or taken from preexisting rock star biographies. These are recipes that were personally given to me by the rock stars in this book. Throughout the writing process, I've had extensive dialogues with these musical hit-makers about their food, on several occasions inquiring with them about tweaks in ingredients or measurements. For me, it has been a very interactive experience.

Writing a cookbook is a whole new experience for me. I have been so excited about compiling every one of these recipes—all of which taste incredible. And how do I know? Because I personally cooked, baked, deep fried, tossed, grilled, and/or boiled every single recipe in this book—and tasting as well as photographing every dish. I am very happy to share with you what has been a true labor of love for me!
What is it like to *Eat Like a Rock Star*? Come along with me—I'm about to show you!

MARK BEGO

ABOUT the Rock & Roll CHEFS

PAUL Antonelli

As one of the founding members of the 1980s band Animotion, keyboard player Paul Antonelli first tasted rock & roll fame via the group's huge international Top Ten 1984 hit: "Obsession." Like so many '80s rock bands, Animotion is best remembered for one single hit recording—and "Obsession" is certainly a great one to have! It was so popular that it not only hit number six in America but was also a Top Ten smash in Canada, New Zealand, Germany, South Africa, and the United Kingdom. In the "Obsession" video, Paul Antonelli is dressed as a sheik, cavorting around a Hollywood Hills swimming pool with his bandmates. A classic shot of Paul in the video finds him regaining consciousness in bed, as though he is waking up from a disco dream. In 1985, Animotion hit the Top 40 with their song "Let Him Go." Since he left the band in the late '80s, Antonelli has become a very much in-demand music supervisor in the world of network TV.

 ANGELA Bowie

Angela Bowie first found fame for having helped mastermind the career of one of rock & roll's '70s legends, her then-husband David Bowie. Together, the duo made up one of the most controversial rock marriages ever, and the androgyny of their costumes and makeup transformed them into the cutting-edge darlings of the rock press. It has long been rumored that Ms. Bowie is the inspiration for The Rolling Stones' song "Angie," and she recorded several of her own cult hits including "The World is Changing." When Angela and David split up in 1976, their divorce made international headlines. It sent Angie off on her own creative path of singing, acting, and writing. In her first book, *Free Spirit* (1981), she introduced the public to her proud admissions of affairs with members of both sexes. Angie also wrote about the possibility of a Mick Jagger-David Bowie affair in her book *Backstage Passes* (1993). She further questioned moral boundaries in society in her books *Lipstick Legends* (2012) and *Pop Sex* (2014).

DEBBY Campbell

The oldest of Glen Campbell's eight children, Debby performed for twenty-four years with her celebrated father in concerts around the world, in residence at The Glen Campbell Theater in Branson, Missouri, and on his live recordings. Not only is she Glen's devoted daughter, she was also his duet partner on their performances of songs like the country hit "Let It Be Me" and the rock classic "United We Stand." She has also been by Glen's side amidst his challenging battle with Alzheimer's disease. Debby told the story of her incredible journey in the touching book *Life with My Father, Glen Campbell* (2014, written with Mark Bego). It hit the Top Ten Best-Seller list in the Nashville newspaper, *The Tennessean*. Although Glen is famous for his many country music hits, many people don't know about his rock & roll history. As a recording session musician in the 1960s, Glen's guitar playing was heard in hits by Elvis Presley, The Beach Boys, The Monkees, The Mamas & The Papas, and Sonny & Cher.

When he was a teenager, Freddy fell in love with rock & roll and dreamed of one day appearing on the famed Dick Clark-hosted TV show *American Bandstand*. In 1959, that is exactly what he did after he penned his own debut hit "Tallahassee Lassie," which hit the US Top Ten and found him making his national television debut. In fact, Freddy has been the most frequent guest in the history of that iconic rock & roll show. He became known as Freddy "Boom Boom" Cannon for his upbeat music, and he produced a long string of hits, including: the Top Ten "Way Down Yonder in New Orleans" (1959), "Jump Over" (1960), "The Urge" (1960), "Transistor Sister" (1961), "Palisades Park" (1963), "Abigail Beecher" (1964), and "Action" (1965), which was the theme song to Dick Clark's mid-'60s rock TV show, *Where the Action Is*. Freddy continues to record and tour. In 2011 Freddy wrote his memoir, *Where the Action Is!*, with Mark Bego, and with an introduction by Dick Clark.

As a rock & roll crooner, Lou has had one of the longest and most impressive careers in the history of the music business. Known for his dramatic string of Top 40 hits–including "The Gypsy Cried," "Two Faces Have I," "I'm Gonna Make You Mine," and "Rhapsody in the Rain"–Lou wrote his own unique songs to showcase his magnificent three-octave range. His ability to effortlessly shift from his normal singing range to his super-sonic upper register falsetto made him an overnight sensation. However, it was his 1966 number one smash "Lightnin' Strikes" that made him a rock superstar. He toured with The Supremes and dozens of other hit makers on Dick Clark's *Caravan of Stars*, and he was regularly seen on such iconic shows as *American Bandstand* and *Where the Action Is*, which made him a teen idol. While millions of fans know him as a singing star, his friends know him as one of the nicest men the rock world. In addition to that, he cooks incredible food!

Two-time Grammy Award-winning songstress Rita Coolidge has one of the most versatile voices in the rock world. She has charted songs on the pop, country, and adult contemporary charts. She first became a star as part of Joe Cocker's phenomenally successful tour and album, *Mad Dogs & Englishmen*. By supplying vocals to the song "Superstar," she literally stopped the show. She was also the inspiration for the Leon Russell song "Delta Lady," and recorded two albums with her then-husband Kris Kristofferson. From 1977 to 1978, she had a string of Top 20 hits, including her versions of Jackie Wilson's "(Your Love Has Lifted Me) Higher and Higher," Boz Scaggs's "We're All Alone," and The Temptations' "The Way You Do the Things You Do." She also scored three number one hits on the adult contemporary charts: "You," "I'd Rather Leave While I'm in Love," and "All Time High," which was the theme from the James Bond film *Octopussy*. In 2016, Rita released her autobiography, *Delta Lady: A Memoir*.

Having had a highly varied career in the music business, Donnie Dacus is known for two prime roles in rock & roll: he was part of the band Chicago in the 1970s, and he was one of the stars of the 1979 film version of *Hair*, playing the role of "Woof" opposite Treat Williams and Beverly D'Angelo. As a guitarist, Donnie has played guitar with a who's who of the rock world, including John Lennon, Boz Scaggs, Billy Joel, Neil Young, Elton John, and Crosby, Stills & Nash. When a spot became available in Chicago, Donnie joined the band in time for its 1978 *Hot Streets* album, which was certified platinum for over a million copies sold. He also recorded on the subsequent *Chicago XIII* album. After two albums with the band, he was suddenly fired, so he simply went off and became part of the band Badfinger. In 2016, after a long time spent away from the band Chicago, Donnie started playing again with some members of the band and was present at Chicago's induction into The Rock & Roll Hall of Fame.

August first became known as one of the original members of the Grammy-nominated disco era-group Dr. Buzzard's Original Savannah Band, before he launched into his second incarnation as the leader of Kid Creole & The Coconuts. Their infectious blend of retro 1940s swing, set to a 1970s disco beat, made them one of 1976's biggest groups, becoming so popular that they were nominated for a "Best New Artist" Grammy Award. The band's signature song, "Cherchez La Femme" is still considered a disco classic. After Dr. Buzzard disbanded, August decided to reinvent himself as a sort of new age Ricky Ricardo/Xavier Cugat type of fictional character, calling himself "Kid Creole." With his trio of background singers, The Coconuts, the band became a success on both sides of the Atlantic with eclectic calypso-influenced rock songs like "Stool Pigeon," "Annie, I'm Not Your Daddy," and "I'm a Wonderful Thing, Baby." In 2016, August co-wrote a play based on "Kid Creole" called *Cherchez La Femme: The Musical*.

As one third of LaBelle—along with Patti LaBelle and Nona Hendryx—Sarah is best known to rock audiences as one of the voices who took the song "Lady Marmalade" to number one in 1976. With their outrageous feathered and spangled silver costumes and their no-holds-barred way of singing, they became rock & roll legends. On their hit albums in the 1970s, they excelled at singing original songs like "(Can I Speak to You Before You Go To) Hollywood" and their own sizzling versions of rock classics like "Wild Horses," "Won't Get Fooled Again," and "Moon Shadow." When the trio broke up, Sarah scored the 1978 Top Ten Dance Hit "Sinner Man." After four successful solo albums, Sarah branched out and sang on The Rolling Stones' *Steel Wheels* album, and then joined her old friend Keith Richards to record several albums as part of his all-star band: The X-Pensive Winos. In 2008, Sarah rejoined Nona and Patti for the LaBelle reunion album *Back to Now* and a concert tour.

Micky first became popular as the child star of the 1950s TV series *Circus Boy*. However, that was just a prelude to his greatest success: as one of The Monkees. Together with Davy Jones, Mike Nesmith, and Peter Tork, Micky found himself caught up in the phenomenally successful TV show–*The Monkees*–and became a bona fide rock & roller along the way. Their 1966 album, *The Monkees*, skyrocketed to number one and sold like hotcakes, as did their next three albums *More of The Monkees*, *Headquarters*, and *Pisces, Aquarius, Capricorn & Jones*. They provided some of the most memorable songs of the decade, including "Last Train to Clarksville," "I'm a Believer," "(I'm Not Your) Stepping Stone," "Pleasant Valley Sunday," and "Daydream Believer." Micky continues to tour with either or both Mike and Peter as The Monkees, and in 2016 they released the Top Ten album *Good Times*. Micky wrote his successful memoir in 1993, *I'm a Believer*, with Mark Bego.

As the lead singer of Dr. Buzzard's Original Savannah Band, Cory Daye is one of the first and most unforgettable divas of the disco era. Singing a blend of retro 1940s big band swing, set to an electronic 1970s disco beat, their self-titled album was such a hit in 1976 that the five-member group was nominated for a Grammy Award as Best New Artist. The band's biggest hit song, "Cherchez La Femme," is considered to be a disco classic, and it is Cory's crystal clear vocals that make the band's sound especially unique. After the individual members of Dr. Buzzard went their separate ways, Cory stayed on RCA Records to record a successful solo album called *Cory & Me*. Utilizing the same retro 1940s sound that made Dr. Buzzard so successful, Cory's singing on that 1979 album went on to create two more hits in the Studio 54 era: "Green Light" and "Pow Wow." Cory Daye still continues to perform her signature '70s hits as part of lavish disco concerts around the globe.

As the lead singer and keyboard player of the rock band Styx, Dennis DeYoung had one of the most familiar voices on the airwaves in the 1970s and 1980s. Having written six out of seven of Styx's Top Ten hits, he was able to infuse his music with his quirky sense of humor. This is best shown on his hit composition "Mr. Roboto," which climbed the charts to number three. The string of Styx Top Ten hits also includes "Show Me the Way," "The Best of Times," "Don't Let it End," "Lady," "Come Sail Away," "Too Much Time on My Hands" (Tommy Shaw composition), and the number one hit "Babe." In 1984, after Shaw exited the band, leaving it in limbo, DeYoung went off and released three solo albums: *Desert Moon* (1984), *Back to the World* (1986), and *Boomchild* (1988). After a Styx reunion from 1990 to 1992, DeYoung started to dabble in acting in rock operas. He played Pontius Pilate on a tour of *Jesus Christ Superstar*, inspiring his 1994 album *10 on Broadway*.

When he moved to California in the 1970s, Walter Egan wanted to get right into the middle of the music business—and that is exactly what he did. Signed to a recording contract, he had originally wanted Brian Wilson of The Beach Boys to

produce his album, but instead he went with Lindsey Buckingham and Stevie Nicks, who were at the height of their success with Fleetwood Mac. This association instantly made Walter's *Fundamental Roll* album a big hit and paved the way for his greatest musical success with the Top Ten hit "Magnet and Steel," featuring both Lindsey and Stevie singing on the song. In fact, it was so popular and radio-friendly that it is often used on soundtrack albums that wish to include a song with a trademark "California sound," including *Boogie Nights* (1997), *Overnight Delivery* (1998), and *Deuce Bigalow: Male Gigolo* (1999). In addition to his string of ten albums, Egan also wrote the song "Hearts on Fire," which was recorded by Gram Parsons.

One of the most beloved singer/ actor/ TV personalities in show business, Joey Fatone enlivens every project he chooses to be involved in. He is most famous for being one fifth of the 1990s and 2000s hit-making group 'N Sync. Along with Lance Bass, Justin Timberlake, Chris Kilpatrick, and JC Chasez, Joey and 'N Sync scored an impressive string of number one hits like "Bye Bye Bye," "It's Gonna Be Me," "Pop," and "Girlfriend." All three of the quintet's studio albums reached number one on the charts: *'N Sync* (Germany), *No Strings Attached*, and *Celebrity* (US and Canada). Since the group broke up, Joey has continued to stay in the public eye in many ways. He was one of the celebrity competitors on TV's *Dancing with the Stars*. He has appeared in movies like *My Big Fat Greek Wedding* and starred in stage productions, such as *The Producers* and *Rock of Ages*. For "foodies," Joey Fatone is also known for his successful runs on several cooking-oriented shows including *My Family Recipe Rocks* and *Rewrapped*.

By the time Duncan Faure joined The Bay City Rollers, the five lads from Scotland already had a string of hits, and so did he! Duncan's original band, Rabbitt, was hugely successful in their native South Africa.

They had a big hit with the song "Charlie" (1976), officially making them local teen idols. When Rabbitt broke up in 1978, fellow band member Trevor Rabin joined the rock group Yes, and Duncan joined The Bay City Rollers. At that time, before Duncan's arrival, The Bay City Rollers had been rocking on since their first hit in 1971, "Keep on Dancing." They had also logged several smashes on the British charts, and "Rollermania" came to the United States via their number one hit "Saturday Night." When a group shake-up occurred, Faure joined the band, and they shortened their name to The Rollers. Duncan proceeded to record three albums with them: *Elevator* (1979), *Voxx* (1980), and *Ricochet* (1981). Duncan also appeared on the Madonna soundtrack album *Who's That Girl* with his song, "24 Hours."

PETE *Filleul*

The Climax Blues Band was one of the most popular British bands in the 1970s and 1980s, and they still perform together. Pete Filleul was their keyboard player from 1970 to 1975, before he rejoined the band from 1977 to 1980. Pete was in the band around the time of their biggest successes, including the hits "Using the Power," "Couldn't Get It Right," "Makin' Love," "I Love You," and "Gotta Have More Love." Their biggest albums were also from the decade that Pete was with the band, including: *Rich Man* (1972), *FM/Live* (1973), *Sense of Direction* (1974), *Stamp Album* (1975), *Gold Plated* (1976), *Shine On* (1978), and *Real to Reel* (1979). Right after *Real to Reel*, Pete left The Climax Blues Band and went on to play with other groups–The Parlour Band, The O Band, and The Blues Band. He later went on to produce a series of movie soundtracks. Filleul can be heard playing keyboards on Loudon Wainwright III's album *40 Odd Years* and The Blues Band's *Back For More*.

DEBBIE *Gibson*

As a teen, Debbie penned her own page in rock and pop music history in 1986 when she wrote, produced, and sang her own number one hit, "Only in My Dreams" at the tender age of sixteen. Debbie Gibson became the youngest singer to have ever accomplished such a feat. A music sensation since she was a little girl on Long Island, it wasn't long before she came to the attention of Atlantic Records, and the rest is history. When her debut album, *Out of the Blue*, was released in 1987, it was certified Triple Platinum. Her follow-up album, *Electric Youth* (1989), spent five weeks at number one in *Billboard*. In 1989, she wrote her first book, *Between the Lines*, with Mark Bego. She is not only known for her Top Ten hits "Shake Your Love," "Only in My Dreams," and the number one "Lost in Your Eyes," but she is also known for her work on Broadway, including playing Eponine in *Les Miserables* in 1992. Debbie and her "rival" Tiffany co-starred in the 2011 sci-fi cult film *Mega Python vs. Gatoroid*.

SUSAYE *Greene*

Susaye is best known for her 1976-77 run as one of The Supremes, replacing departing Cindy Birdsong in the group. She appeared on the trio's pair of disco era albums: *High Energy* and *Mary, Scherrie & Susaye*. Possessing a multi-octave singing range, she can be heard on several of The Supremes prime cuts of the era, including "High Energy" and "You're My Driving Wheel." Susaye had come to The Supremes highly recommended by Stevie Wonder; Susaye was already part of the Motown world as a member of Stevie's background group, Wonderlove. She was also prominently featured on the song "Joy Inside My Tears" from Wonder's number one hit album *Songs in the Key of Life* (1976). In 1977, The Supremes broke up. Mary Wilson started her solo career, and Susaye joined Scherrie Payne to record their Motown duet album, *Partners* (1979). Susaye and Stevie Wonder co-wrote the song "I Can't Help It" for Michael Jackson, which appears on his multi-platinum *Off the Wall* album.

From the very beginning of the legendary rock group Three Dog Night in 1968 right up to 2014, Jimmy Greenspoon was a faithful member. In the 1970s, Three Dog Night, a septet with three lead singers and four musicians, was one of the top ten highest earning and best-selling rock bands in the world. From the very start of their long and multimillion-selling recording career, they racked up an incredible string of Top Ten hits, including "One (Is the Loneliest Number)," "Easy to Be Hard," "Eli's Comin'," "Mama Told Me Not to Come," "An Old Fashioned Love Song," "Joy to the World," "Never Been to Spain," "Black & White," and "The Show Must Go On." As the keyboard player in the group, it was Jimmy Greenspoon who created the elaborate intros and solos for Three Dog Night's songs. His revealing rock & roll autobiography, *One Is the Loneliest Number* (written with Mark Bego), was first published in 1991. Sadly, while this book was being written, Jimmy passed away in March 2015 of cancer.

In rock & roll terms, Balázs Havasi is the Elton John of Hungary. Both men were proficient at the piano from an early age, and each of them have let exciting music and flashy showmanship define their musical careers. Musically, Havasi's compositions are very grand and keyboard-driven, with rock guitars and dramatic drumming that has had Europe fascinated with his music. In Hungary, Havasi draws huge crowds at his concerts. To break through to the British rock audience, Havasi founded the band The Unbending Trees, which released its first album in 2007, featuring Havasi's piano playing and Christóf Hajós singing. Recently at The Papp Laszlo Sports Arena in Budapest, lightning-fingered Havasi drew crowds of over 46,000 people to see him perform. Havasi's series of albums have included: *Confessions on Piano* (2001), *Sounds of the Heart* (2003), *Days and Nights* (2004), *Infinity* (2007), *Red* (2010), and *Drum & Piano* (2011). In 2015, Havasi made his American concert debut at Carnegie Hall in New York City.

There are times in the music business where an incredible singer is best remembered for a single song even though they have recorded a huge body of great music. Grammy Award-winning songstress Thelma Houston is one of these. She is best known for her number one hit "Don't Leave Me This Way," but her very active career encompasses so much more. She was first heard singing with The Art Reynolds Singers. When their song "Jesus Is Just Alright" became a hit for The Doobie Brothers, rock fans started taking notice. Thelma recorded her first solo album, *Sunshower* (1969), as the musical protégée of singer/songwriter Jimmy Webb. It included her brilliant take on The Rolling Stones' "Jumpin' Jack Flash." When she signed with Motown Records, things really began to sizzle for her. Her 1974 single "You've Been Doing Wrong for So Long" garnered her a Grammy nomination and directly led her into her unforgettable 1977 disco smash "Don't Leave Me This Way."

TOMMY *James*

Coming from Niles, Michigan, Tommy James formed his own band, The Shondells, in 1964, and they recorded the song "Hanky Panky." Signed to Snap Records, the song did well in Michigan and the surrounding area. Having seen only local success, the band broke up. Suddenly a Pittsburgh dance promoter starting playing the song at events, and the next thing he knew, Tommy James had a hit on his hands. Without the first batch of Shondells to back him up in concert, Tommy recast the band, and the rechristened Tommy James & The Shondells not only hit number one with "Hanky Panky" (1966), they also did it again with "Crimson and Clover" (1968). Along the way, Tommy and his band had a long string of hit songs including "Say What I Am" (1966), "I Think We're Alone Now" (1967), "Mirage" (1967), "Gettin' Together" (1967), "Mony Mony" (1968), "Sweet Cherry Wine" (1969), and "Crystal Blue Persuasion" (1969). In 1971, Tommy released the solo hit "Draggin' the Line."

Before he became known as the original cowboy in the group The Village People, Randy Jones was an accomplished dancer. When he joined The Village People in 1978, he was

RANDY *Jones*

instantly taken into the recording studio to create several of the biggest hit songs that defined the whole disco era: "Macho Man," "In the Navy," "Can't Stop the Music," and the iconic "Y.M.C.A." As part of The Village People, Randy toured the world, bringing disco music to the masses. To date, the group The Village People has sold more than 100 million record albums and singles. In 1980, Randy and the other members of the group starred in their own semi-autobiographical cult-worshipped disco movie, *Can't Stop the Music*. Since leaving The Village People in the 1990s, Randy has produced his own solo albums. In 2008, he published the book *Macho Man: The Disco Era and Gay America's Coming Out* (with Mark Bego). Randy Jones was one of the stars of the 2014 film *Tales of Poe*, and he released the album *Mister Right* in 2016.

BETTY *Kelly*

In the mid-sixties, Betty Kelly became part of a Motown legendary act when she replaced Annette Beard in the hit-making group Martha & The Vandellas, singing and recording with Martha Reeves and Rosalind Ashford in the famed girl group trio. She was on three of the group's most popular albums: *Watchout!*, *Martha & The Vandellas Live!*, and *Ridin' High*. Her voice can be heard on the trio's smash hits "Dancing in the Street," "Jimmy Mack," "I'm Ready for Love," and "Honey Chile." Betty's beauty and effervescent personality have made her one of the most beloved singers in Vandella history. She currently lives in Los Angeles, California, and she lights up the room when she attends high profile musical events and key Motown gatherings. She can not only sing beautifully but also cook delicious food, too! Betty lends her time to charitable causes and actively participates at the annual HAL (Heroes and Legends) Awards, which gives music scholarships to young aspiring musicians.

Sean Lennon was literally born in the middle of the rock world. The son of John Lennon and Yoko Ono, his childhood was immortalized in the song "Beautiful Boy" by his father, and he has been the musical director of his mom's resurrected

Plastic Ono Band. Today, Sean has his own rock band called The Ghost of a Saber Tooth Tiger (aka Ghostt), which he fronts with his girlfriend and musical collaborator, Charlotte Kemp Muhl. Together, they have released three albums of music: *Ghost of a Saber Tooth Tiger: The Acoustic Sessions* (2010), *La Carotte Bleue* (2011), and the psychedelic-sounding *Midnight Sun* (2014). As a solo artist, Lennon has also recorded and released several albums: *Into the Sun* (1998), *Half Horse, Half Musician* (1999), *Friendly Fire* (2006), and the original soundtrack recordings to the films *Rosencrantz and Guildernstern Are Undead* (2009) and *Alter Egos* (2012). In 2016, he released the psychedelic *Monolith with Phobos* with Les Claypool as The Claypool Lennon Delirium.

In the 1960s, The Fifth Dimension became one of the most active hit-making vocal groups in the rock and pop world. Marilyn McCoo and her husband, Billy Davis Jr., were two of the five original members in that incredible quintet. Along with their bandmates Florence LaRue Gordon, Ron Townsend, and Lamonte McLemore, they first hit the Top Ten with their 1967 hit "Up, Up and Away," and they continued to record smash after smash, including "Stoned Soul Picnic," "Last Night I Didn't Get to Sleep at All," and a series of number ones like "Never My Love," "One Less Bell to Answer," and the psychedelic era classic "Aquarius / Let the Sunshine In." In 1975, Marilyn and Billy left The Fifth Dimension, and in 1976 they recorded the hit "You Don't Have to Be a Star (to Be in My Show)," which earned them their seventh Grammy Award. Always popular on television, Marilyn took over as the host of the hit musical TV show *Solid Gold* from 1981 to 1984. She and Billy continue to tour as a duet.

Possessing one of the most distinctive and rich voices in all of rock and pop music, Michael McDonald is best

known as a former member of The Doobie Brothers, helping to bring that band to its greatest Grammy Award–winning commercial successes. Earlier in his career, in 1974, Michael joined the touring band of Steely Dan, and he also appeared on their albums *Katy Lied, The Royal Scam, Aja,* and *Gaucho.* In 1975 he was recruited by The Doobie Brothers when original member Tom Johnston dropped out. He fit in so well with the band that he became a permanent member, and he was first featured on their 1976 album *Takin' It to the Streets.* He sang the lead vocals on their hits "It Keeps You Runnin,'" "Minute by Minute," "Little Darling (I Need You)," and the number one smash "What a Fool Believes." In 1982, Michael released his solo album *If That's What It Takes*. He has been a rock & roll headliner ever since. In 1979, a book about the band and Michael McDonald, *The Doobie Brothers*, was written by Mark Bego.

Not to be confused with *Our Gang* movie actor Spanky McFarland, Elaine "Spanky" McFarlane is the dynamic female voice of the '60s and '70s rock band Spanky & Our Gang, which produced a string of six Top 40 hits, including "Sunday Will Never Be the Same," "Making Every Minute Count," "Lazy Day," "Sunday Mornin'," "Like to Get to Know You," and the protest song "Give a Damn." They were also the originators of the 1969 song "Echoes (Everybody's Talkin')" that was made famous the next year by Harry Nilsson. Possessing a voice that is very similar to that of Mama Cass Elliot, Spanky began filling in for the late Cass beginning in the 1980s in the second incarnation of The Mamas & The Papas (along with John Phillips, Denny Doherty, and Mackenzie Phillips filling in for Michelle Phillips). Although the members in the rock band Our Gang perpetually evolved, Spanky joined two of her former original band members for a one-night-only Spanky & Our Gang reunion in 1999.

One of the most gracious and lovely ladies in all of rock & roll, Melanie will always be known as one of the top stars of the 1969 Woodstock festival. Her first Top Ten hit, "Lay Down (Candles in

the Rain)," is a song she wrote about being at Woodstock where the crowd lit candles to illuminate her performance. While most people know Melanie for her infectious 1972 number one worldwide hit "Brand New Key," she has scored several international Top Ten hits in her long and glorious career, including "Peace Will Come According to Plan," "Look What They've Done to My Song, Ma," "Ring the Living Bell," "Together Alone," and her brilliant interpretation of The Rolling Stones' "Ruby Tuesday." She can be heard on the *Woodstock Two* album from that iconic tie-dyed rock & roll musical love fest, singing her passionate songs "My Beautiful People" and "Birthday of the Sun." Melanie won an Emmy Award in 1989 for her lyrics to the song "The First Time I Loved Forever," from the TV series *Beauty & The Beast*.

As the lead singer of the 1980s band Berlin, Terri Nunn's voice is most famous for the song "Take My Breath Away," which appeared on the soundtrack of the film *Top Gun* as its love theme. The song went on to hit number one and cemented Nunn into rock & roll fame. Having joined the band in 1978, Terri then went off to pursue an acting career, but rejoined Berlin in 1981. In addition to their trademark song, Terri and Berlin's string of hits include "The Metro,"

"No More Words," "You Don't Know," "Masquerade," and "Sex (I'm a...)." As an actress, Nunn was in the disco film *Thank God It's Friday* (1978) and several TV series, such as *T. J. Hooker*, *Lou Grant*, and *James at 15*. Terri left Berlin in 1986 and recorded the song "Dancing in Isolation" for the film *Better Off Dead*. In 1996, Terri gained the rights to the band name *Berlin* and reformed the group around herself. The original band came together in 2003 for the VH1 series, *Bands Reunited*. Terri and Berlin recorded a live album in 2009.

Born in Detroit, Ray started playing the guitar when he was still a teenager. He was in the house band at The 20 Grand nightclub, playing behind such famed Motown stars as The Temptations, The Spinners, Gladys Knight & the Pips, and Stevie Wonder. When Ray was just eighteen, he was asked by Stevie to go on the road with him for his tour with The Rolling Stones. Ray did just that, and he also played guitar on Wonder's two most iconic albums, *Talking Book* and *Innervisions*. Signed to Arista Records in 1977, Ray and his group Raydio began producing hits, including "Jack and Jill" and "You Can't Change That." As a solo artist, Ray continued to hit the charts with songs like "A Woman Needs Love (Just Like You Do)" and "The Other Woman." However, when the movie theme song "Ghostbusters" hit number one on the Pop and R&B charts, he instantly had his signature song. Ray Parker Jr. continues to play his distinctive guitar on hit albums for recording stars like Michael McDonald, Van Morrison, and Boz Scaggs.

In the world of rock & roll, pop, and soul, Freda will always be remembered for her infectiously appealing 1970 hit song, "Band of Gold," which hit number one in Great Britain and number three in the US. Signed to Eddie Holland, Lamont Dozier, and Brian Holland's Detroit-based post-Motown label, Invictus Records, Freda recorded four memorable albums, including *Band of Gold, Contact, The Best of Freda Payne*, and *Reaching Out*. She became an international star with several of her singles on the Top 40 charts in the US and UK. She scored big with the songs "Bring the Boys Home," "Deeper and Deeper," "Cherish What Is Dear to You (While It's Near to You)," and "You Brought the Joy." When she signed with Capitol Records in 1977, Freda released a trio of successful disco albums, as well as the hit single "Love Magnet." In 2011, Freda recorded the song "Saving a Life" with British pop star Sir Cliff Richard for his *Soulicious* album in 2011 and released her own jazz album *Come Back to Me Love* in 2014.

Most well known as a member of The Supremes from 1974 to 1977, Scherrie has been singing all her life. She started out as the lead singer for the Detroit group Glass House. They were signed to Invictus Records, the same label at which Scherrie's sister, Freda, recorded. Glass House and Scherrie had one big hit song there, "Crumbs off the Table." When Jean Terrell dropped out of The Supremes in 1973, Scherrie joined Mary Wilson and Cindy Birdsong in the famed trio at Motown Records. The trio's first Supremes single became a hit and a fan favorite: "He's My Man," with lead singing by Scherrie and Mary. It was the group's 1976 album, *High Energy*, that gave the trio their final Top 40 hit single, the disco smash, "I'm Gonna Let My Heart Do the Walking." For the band's next and final album, *Mary, Scherrie & Susaye*, Cindy had dropped out and was replaced by Susaye Greene. When The Supremes disbanded in 1977, Scherrie and Susaye recorded a duet album on Motown Records called *Partners*.

The lovely Michelle has had one of the most varied careers in rock & roll. As one of The Mamas & The Papas— along with John Phillips, Denny Doherty, and Cass Elliot—Michelle first found fame in 1965 with the huge Top Ten hit "California Dreamin'," and the band quickly followed it up with the number one "Monday, Monday." It was Michelle's beautiful solo voice that came lilting over the airwaves when the quartet released their smashing 1967 hit "Dedicated to the One I Love." By the 1970s, the band members had gone their separate ways, and Michelle became one of the most popular actresses in Hollywood, landing roles in the films *Valentino* and *Dillinger*. As the third act to her career, Michelle joined the cast of the hit TV show *Knots Landing* in the 1980s and the cast of *Beverly Hills 90210* in the '90s. She is the mother of Wilson Phillips's songstress Chynna Phillips. Michelle is one of the most beloved women to be inducted in the Rock & Roll Hall of Fame.

As one of the most famous women in the rock & roll world, Reeves became an international star via her ten-year recording career at Motown Records as the lead singer of Martha & The Vandellas. With their incredible string of hit singles in the 1960s through to the 1970s, the trio is beloved for their Top Ten hits "Dancing in the Street," "Heat Wave," "Jimmy Mack," "Nowhere to Run," and "I'm Ready For Love." They were also hot on the charts with "Honey Chile," "Come and Get These Memories," and the heartfelt ballad "My Baby Loves Me." After she left Motown Records, Reeves signed with MCA Records and proceeded to record one of the most legendary albums of the decade, *Martha Reeves*, produced by Richard Perry and featuring guest stars, such as James Taylor, Hoyt Axton, and Billy Preston. It was the most expensive album ever produced at that time. In 1994 Martha published her memoir *Dancing in the Street: Confessions of a Motown Diva* (with Mark Bego), which became a Top Ten *Chicago Tribune* best-seller.

RICHIE *Sambora*

A true rock star guitarist, Richie first found superstardom in the band Bon Jovi. As the flashy and accomplished lead guitarist in the group, Richie proved he was born for the spotlight. His guitar playing was heavily influenced by Eric Clapton, Jeff Beck, Johnny Winter, and Stevie Ray Vaughn. His first professional gig came in the early 1980s as the opening act to Joe Cocker. Just before he joined Bon Jovi, Richie had auditioned to be Ace Frehley's replacement in Kiss. When he teamed up with Jon Bon Jovi, Sambora and the band recorded some of the most defining rock & roll anthems of the '80s, including "Wanted Dead or Alive" and "You Give Love a Bad Name." Sambora has also found his personal life very much a subject of tabloid headlines. Married to actress Heather Locklear, his 1980s love affair with Cher pushed him even further into the spotlight. He is currently dating fellow guitar-playing pro, Orianthi. Since leaving Bon Jovi, Richie has recorded a string of solo albums, including *Aftermath of the Lowdown* in 2012.

BOZ *Scaggs*

Boz Scaggs has been a rock star since 1976, when he released his breakthrough album, the five-million-selling *Silk Degrees*, which reached number one in several countries. Since then, he has gone on to branch out into synthesizer rock on *Other Roads* (1988), rhythm & blues on *Come on Home* (1997), and incredible interpretations of classic jazz standards on *But Beautiful* (2003) and *Speak Low* (2008). In 2013, Boz decided to do an album comprised of blues-oriented songs. Scaggs journeyed to the South to make one of his most brilliant albums yet, entitled *Memphis*. Recorded at Royal Studios in Memphis, where Willie Mitchell once created the biggest hits of Al Green's career, Boz discovered "magic" in the air and found himself possessed and inspired by it. His latest album, 2015's *A Fool to Care*, follows that same blues/rock feeling and includes duets with Lucinda Williams and the great Bonnie Raitt. Scaggs is also the owner of his own vineyard north of San Francisco; and he cooks, too!

JAY *Siegel*

As one of the members of The Tokens, Jay and his bandmates hit number one in 1961 with their iconic song "The Lion Sleeps Tonight," featuring Siegel's show-stopping falsetto voice. The band had originally formed in Brooklyn, New York, in 1955, calling themselves The Linc-Tones and featuring future pop star Neil Sedaka. When group member Eddie Rabkin dropped out of the band in 1956, it was Siegel who took his place, where he has been for an amazing sixty years. The band has become a revolving door for subsequent members since then, but there has always been a group of The Tokens. In 1961, the group's song "Tonight I Fell in Love" made it to Number 15 on the US charts, and they were booked to appear on rock's most famous TV show, *American Bandstand*. That made quite a sensation and led to them releasing their follow-up single, "The Lion Sleeps Tonight." When it hit number one, The Tokens cemented their place in music history. Siegel continues to perform in concert.

Someone who has always filled her career with lots of excitement, gusto, and drama, Jade is internationally known as the lead singer of the 1980s rock band Pretty Poison. The band scored a huge Top Ten hit in 1987

with the song "Catch Me (I'm Falling)," which cemented their place in '80s rock history. Their subsequent singles, "Nighttime" and "When I Look in Your Eyes," continued to keep them hot on the charts during this same era. Like so many concerned rock stars, Jade Starling has put her time and energy behind several charities and causes that she finds dear to her heart. An outspoken supporter of gay rights and same-sex marriage, Jade has also performed at fundraisers for Hurricane Sandy victims and whatever worthy causes pique her interest. Since embarking on a solo recording career, Jade has released several danceable recordings, including her exciting and edgy album *Captive* (2014). Jade Starling's singing is bold and exciting, and so is her cooking.

Known as one fourth of the 1990s Motown vocal group Boyz II Men, along with band members Michael McCary, Nathan Morris, and Wanya Morris,

Shawn first found massive fame with their 1992 hit "End of the Road," which hit number one in *Billboard* magazine and reigned there for thirteen weeks, breaking a record previously set by Elvis Presley. They then went on to break that record two more times, first with their song "I'll Make Love to You," which was number one for fourteen weeks, and their duet with Mariah Carey, "One Sweet Day," which was number one for sixteen weeks. Their song "On Bended Knee" also hit number one on the charts. McCary dropped out of the band in 2003, and they continue to perform as a trio. In 2007, Boyz II Men released an album entitled *Motown: A Journey Through Hitsville USA*, which found them doing a fitting tribute to the famed Detroit record label that made them famous, and it hit the UK Top Ten. Shawn was a judge on the TV talent show *The Sing-Off* from 2009 to 2014.

Originally labeled the teen queen of shopping mall singing, at the age of sixteen she scored her first number one hit with her dramatic version of the Tommy James & The Shondell's

classic "I Think We're Alone Now." In February 1988, Tiffany scored her second number one hit with the ballad "Could've Been," causing her debut album to sell in excess of 4.1 million copies. A third single, her own version of The Beatles' "I Saw Her Standing There," retooled to become "I Saw Him Standing There," became a Top Ten hit for her as well. Although her teenage days were dramatically successful for her on the record charts, Tiffany is someone who has never stopped growing and stretching in her career. She provided the voice for Judy Jetson in the animated film *Jetsons: The Movie* (1990), starred with Debbie Gibson in the SyFy Channel's camp classic film *Mega Python vs. Gatoroid* (2011), and recorded a country album called *Rose Tattoo*. She moved to Nashville and opened her own vintage clothing store.

TANYA *Tucker*

Born in Texas and raised in Arizona, Tanya Tucker was performing in talent competitions as a child and had her first public gig at the Arizona State Fair. Country legend Mel Tillis was the first star to discover her and let her perform with him, which brought record company recognition. She scored her first Top Ten country hit, "Delta Dawn," in 1972 when she was thirteen years old. Producing smashes on both the Country and Pop music charts, Tanya has racked up dozens of hits, including "Down to My Last Teardrop," "Walking Shoes," and "It's a Little Too Late." In 1978, at the age of nineteen she released her first full-out rock & roll album, *T-N-T*, which found her tackling Buddy Holly's "Not Fade Away," John Prine's "Angel From Montgomery," and Elvis Presley's "Heartbreak Hotel." One of Tanya's most exciting rock & roll recordings is her red-hot rendition of "Already Gone" on the triple Platinum album *Common Thread: The Songs of The Eagles* in 1993. She is truly one of the most exciting singing stars around!

CHERRY *Vanilla*

Having first found fame as an actress in the London cast of Andy Warhol's avant garde play *Pork* in the early 1970s, Cherry Vanilla is a legendary part of the whole Warhol/Bowie downtown scene. While in the cast of the play, she met David and Angela Bowie, and was hired by Bowie's NYC based company, MainMan, as its innovative Head of Publicity. She was so good at garnering publicity for Bowie that she next turned her talents to her own career. With her trademark cherry-red hair, she formed her own band and became a high profile draw as a singer and songwriter. When she relocated to London, she became a fixture of the growing punk scene and in 1976 was signed to RCA Records. Cherry's band in London included Stuart Copeland and his friend Gordon "Sting" Sumner, who later went out on their own as two-thirds of The Police. Vanilla's first album, *Bad Girl*, was released in 1978, followed by *Venus D'Vinyl* in 1979. In 2010, she released her frank memoir, *Lick Me: How I Became Cherry Vanilla*.

MARI *Wilson*

British songbird Mari Wilson (not to be confused with The Supremes' Mary Wilson) first became a hit on the British music charts in 1982 with her first two singles, "Beat the Beat" and "Baby It's True." However, it was her third single, "Just What I Always Wanted," that became her biggest Top Ten smash. She released her debut album, *Showpeople*, the following year, and between her infectious pop influenced sound and her retro '60s look and trademark beehive hairdo, she caused a huge media stir. She was able to score three more hits from that same album: "(Beware) Boyfriend," her version of "Cry Me a River," and "Wonderful to Be with You." In 1985, Mari recorded the theme song for the film *Dance with a Stranger*. With her 1991 album *The Rhythm Romance*, she began to delve into more of a pop/jazz style. Her 2016 album, *Pop Deluxe*, features Mari in her retro '60s mode, featuring the songs of Petula Clark, Dusty Springfield, and Brazil '66, as well as Gene Pitney's "24 Hours From Tulsa."

As one third of the world-famous Supremes, Mary Wilson, along with Florence Ballard and Diana Ross, recorded a string of number one singles that became some of the most memorable and enduring songs that  made up the soundtrack of the 1960s, such as "Baby Love," "Stop! In the Name of Love," and "The Happening." With new members Jean Terrell and Cindy Birdsong in the 1970s, Mary and The Supremes continued to score hit after hit, including "Up the Ladder to the Roof," "Stoned Love," and "Floy Joy." A solo performer since 1979, Mary continues to tour the globe as a top performer, equally adept at delivering the Motown Sound, exciting ballads, emotionally touching jazz, and rock & roll. Mary is also the author of two best-selling memoirs: *Dreamgirl: My Life as a Supreme* and *Supreme Faith: Someday We'll Be Together*. She continues to tour the globe presenting her Supremes show, her poignant jazz show, and her rock & roll show. Mark Bego is often along for the ride!

 Bill Wyman became a rock legend as the original bass player in The Rolling Stones, and he is now known as the leader of his all-star band The Rhythm Kings. Bill joined The Stones in 1962 and appeared on every one of the band's international number one hits from "I Can't Get No Satisfaction" up to "Miss You." He was in the band from the very beginning, right up through the recording of the 1989 *Steel Wheels* album and the subsequent world concert tour that bore the same name. Wanting to pursue his own music, Bill officially left The Rolling Stones in 1993 and rounded up several of his favorite fellow musicians to record and play with him in a group billed as "Bill Wyman's Rhythm Kings." Their recordings and tours have been a huge success. Bill's lifelong love of art and photography has blossomed into having his historic rock & roll photos displayed in several international galleries, including in Monte Carlo. In the food arena, he also the owner of three Sticky Fingers Cafés in England.

Breakfast & Brunch

Nutritionists claim that breakfast is the most important meal of the day. With the recipes in this chapter, it can also be the most rocking meal of the day, too. If eggs are your thing, Mary Wilson's Caviar Omelet (page 14) is exciting and decadent, Tommy James' Niles, Michigan, Omelet (page 12) gives bacon a starring role, and Ray Parker Jr.'s Salmon & Eggs (page 2) are absolutely delicious. If baking is your thing, try Debbie Gibson's Coconut Biscuits (page 10) or my Key Lime Coconut Donuts (page 16). These plates make getting out of bed truly worthwhile!

Credit: Derek Storm

Credit: MJB Photo Archives

LEFT: I have known Debbie Gibson since she was a teenager. She has since blossomed into a rock star, a talented actress, and an incredible cook!
RIGHT: Ray Parker Jr. and I at my favorite Malibu seafood restaurant, The Reel Inn, where we discuss his rocking musical career over fish and chips.

Salmon, Eggs & Grits
RAY PARKER JR.

I never thought of using canned salmon in such a creative way, and it tastes great with a little sauté to crisp and brown. The salmon is a perfect match with eggs and grits. This recipe is in fact from Ray's wife, Elaine Parker, and it is his all-time morning meal of choice. As Ray said, "This is my favorite breakfast. I have it all the time!"

YIELD:

SERVES 2 HUNGRY PEOPLE

INGREDIENTS

1 cup water

¼ cup grits (the "five minute" variety)

4 to 6 eggs

1 tablespoon butter or olive oil

1 can (6 oz) skinless boneless salmon

1 scallion or 6 sprigs chives, chopped (about ¼ cup)

¼ teaspoon sea salt

¼ teaspoon ground black pepper

OPTIONAL:

Fresh fruit to serve with it: blueberries, raspberries, kiwi, peaches, watermelon, cantaloupe, grapes, strawberries . . . the sky is the limit!

Boil 1 cup water. When it reaches a boil, stir in the grits, reduce to low heat, and simmer for 5 to 7 minutes, or until thickened. Elaine suggests, "Grits: Make according to directions, but add a little bit more water (¼ to ⅓ cup) because Ray likes his grits thin, not thick!"

Whisk eggs (optional: for fluffier eggs: add ¼ cup milk). Optional spice additions: salt, pepper, paprika, garlic powder. Set aside until the salmon is ready.

Using either butter or olive oil, over medium high heat in a frying pan, sauté the salmon for 2 minutes to heat it up and brown it a touch. According to Elaine: "Continue sautéing, then add whisked eggs. Continue stirring and scrambling eggs with the salmon. Just before it's done, add in chopped scallions or chives, continue stirring, and add in sea salt and pepper." She also instructs: "Ray likes his eggs browned, so I cook them well done!"

Elaine suggests: "Serve salmon/eggs on a plate with grits on the side . . . grits with a pat of butter and salt and pepper. Garnish with fruit that is in season."

If you are going to invite everyone's favorite Ghostbuster—Ray Parker Jr.—over for breakfast, this is how he likes to start his day!

Dr. Mary's Grits Casserole
MARILYN MCCOO OF THE FIFTH DIMENSION

The minute Marilyn McCoo mentioned this recipe to me, I instantly had a premonition that it was going to be a winner, as well as a wonderful addition to the breakfast section of this book. So many people love grits but don't know how to prepare them. Well, your wait is over! Like all of her recipes, this is dedicated to someone special to her. As Marilyn said, "Everyone called my mother Dr. Mary, and this is her recipe. This is a great dish to make for a brunch! This recipe is in memory of my mother; it's always a crowd pleaser."

YIELD:
SERVES 10 TO 12 PEOPLE

INGREDIENTS
2 teaspoons salt
8 cups water (for preparing grits)
2 cups grits
3 eggs
1 stick butter or margarine
2 teaspoons dried parsley flakes
1 lb grated or sliced Cheddar cheese
½ cup fresh chopped parsley (for optional garnish)

DIRECTIONS

Put the salt into water and boil the water. Slowly stir the grits into the boiling water, stirring constantly to prevent clumping. I have found that stirring the grits with a wire whisk is the best way to prevent them from getting lumpy. Turn the heat down and continue to cook for 6-7 minutes.

Preheat oven to 350°F. Crack eggs into a bowl, whisk together, and set aside. After 5 to 6 minutes of the grits cooking, remove the pot from the heat and add the butter or margarine and the dried parsley flakes. Stir the butter or margarine until it fully melts. Slowly pour the beaten eggs into the grits, and stir them in with a whisk. Pour the grits mixture into a large baking pan.

Take half of the grated Cheddar cheese (8 oz) and cover the grits. With a spoon, swirl and submerge the cheese into the hot grits. Take the other half of the grated Cheddar cheese and cover the top of the grits.

Put the casserole into the preheated oven, and bake for 30 to 35 minutes. According to Marilyn, "Bake 'til the cheese has melted and casserole is bubbling."

You can optionally garnish the grits with fresh chopped parsley, either in the baking pan or on individual servings on the plate.

NOTE: Just like Marilyn recommends, this is an incredible casserole for a brunch or a breakfast buffet. Additionally, I have also found that this is an amazing dish to serve with pan-fried shrimp to turn it into a dinner main course of "Shrimp and Grits." Take 1 lb shrimp, add salt, ground black pepper, and cayenne pepper, and pan-fry them in olive oil for 5 minutes. Serve on top of the grits.

Ultimate Breakfast Smoothie
TERRI NUNN OF BERLIN

Terri Nunn claims, "I've never been one who ate fruit much. Yet I know the health advantages. This smoothie has stood the test of time for me and all my kids. It's easy and they love it—never get tired of it. We get our sweet tooth satisfied and a day's full serving of fruit, without added refined sugar. The secret that makes this one different is the dates. They naturally sweeten it, and, when soaked with the smoothie, they taste like candy in the drink! Yum!"

YIELD:
2 SMOOTHIES

INGREDIENTS
2 sliced bananas
1½ cups berries (strawberries, blackberries, raspberries, or other fruit)
2 cups orange juice
¼ cup pitted and chopped dates

DIRECTIONS

"Cut up the bananas into small pieces," Terri instructs. "Cut up the fruit if you need to. Raspberries, mango, blackberries, strawberries—especially frozen strawberries—work great and don't need cutting up."

Pour the orange juice into the blender. Add the bananas. Then add the additional fruit.

Terri says, "Lastly throw in the dates. Blend on medium high for 20 to 30 seconds. If too slushy, pause blender, stir around, and restart. Pour into glasses. I like to add extra date pieces on top too. Enjoy!"

NOTE: Terri has some definite ideas about the ingredients that go into making her Ultimate Smoothie. With regard to orange juice, she suggests, "preferably fresh, but any will do." Sometimes she puts the bananas in the freezer before she adds them to the smoothies. According to her, "Frozen ones make it like a slushy! Fresh ones are fine, too."

Shrimp Frittata
ANGELA BOWIE

According to Angela, "This is the perfect recipe if you are setting up a 'breakfast buffet' for several people." Take it from the exciting Ms. Bowie–this recipe is a show stopper. It could also be served at cocktail hour as a Spanish tapas bar-style Tortilla Espanola.

YIELD:

SERVES 8 TO 10 PEOPLE

INGREDIENTS

12 to 15 shrimp

10 eggs

½ cup whole milk

½ teaspoon salt

½ teaspoon ground black pepper

¼ cup olive oil

½ cup chopped onion

½ cup chopped red pepper

½ cup sliced leek

½ cup sliced mushrooms

1 cup chopped spinach

DIRECTIONS

Remove the shells and tails from the shrimp, and either boil them for three minutes or pan fry them. Remove from heat and set aside. When they have cooled off, slice them in half or into smaller pieces.

In a mixing bowl, add the eggs, milk, salt, and pepper. Whisk them together and set aside. Preheat the oven to 350°F.

In a cast iron frying pan, add olive oil and onions, red peppers and sliced leeks. Sauté them until they start to soften and brown, then add the mushrooms. At the end, add the spinach and stir it in, just enough to wilt it. Add the shrimp to the frying pan, and arrange everything evenly in it.

Pour the beaten eggs into the cast iron frying pan and continue to cook for 5 to 7 minutes. As it starts to get done, you will see the outer edge of the eggs pulling away from the sides of the pan. At this point, place the frying pan into the preheated oven and bake for 15 to 20 minutes.

The desired effect is to see some browning on the top surface of the eggs. Remove from the oven. You can either flip the frittata onto a large flat plate or serve it from the wrought iron frying pan with a spatula. Slice it like a pie or a quiche, and serve alongside fresh fruit, salad, or any other breakfast/brunch accompaniment.

NOTE: The perfect—and traditional—pan for making frittatas is a 10-inch cast iron frying pan, as it will go on the stove and then into the oven. However, you can also make this in a 2-quart glass baking pan and bake it in the oven. In a glass pan, baking time will vary with the thickness of the frittata, from 20 to 30 minutes.

Coconut Biscuits
DEBBIE GIBSON

These are so easy to make, and they are so good. Furthermore, they are totally vegan (unless you smear them with butter, which you are strongly advised to do). Personally, I love these with orange marmalade!

YIELD:

APPROXIMATELY 12 BISCUITS

INGREDIENTS

2 cups self-rising flour*
2 tablespoons sugar**
¼ cup coconut oil (solid, not melted)
¾ cup unsweetened coconut milk (or any milk)

* If you don't have self-rising flour, combine 2 cups flour, 4 teaspoons baking powder, and ¼ teaspoon baking soda.

** Instead of sugar, Debbie's original recipe asks to use ½ teaspoon of "Dr. Rutledge's SweetyHi" low-calorie sweetener. It can be found on the Internet. Both the sugar and the sweetener work equally well.

DIRECTIONS
Preheat oven to 425°F.

Mix the self-rising flour (or regular flour, baking powder, and baking soda), sugar (or sweetener), and coconut oil in a mixing bowl. As Debbie instructs, "Using a fork, make a cutting motion until the mixture looks like crumbs. Stir in the milk until the mixture forms into a soft dough and does not stick to the bowl."

"Dust a cutting board lightly with flour, and roll the dough onto the cutting board into ½-inch thickness," says Debbie. If you are using a biscuit cutter or round cookie cutter, "Cut dough into 2 inch circles and transfer to a lightly greased baking sheet." If you are *not* using a biscuit cutter, Debbie advises, "Simply take the dough and roll it into desired shapes and sizes, and put onto a lightly greased baking sheet." Parchment paper is also perfect for these biscuits, instead of greasing the pan. Bake the coconut biscuits for 10 minutes or until the tops of the biscuits brown and you see that the dough has risen.

According to Debbie Gibson: "Cut in the middle, and add some butter to taste if so desired! Serve *hot*!"

Niles, Michigan, Omelet
TOMMY JAMES OF THE SHONDELLS

Tommy–of Tommy James & The Shondells–names his favorite omelet after his hometown of Niles, Michigan. He not only mapped out the recipe for the eggs but also designed the ultimate "Tommy James Breakfast." He likes this served with an English muffin, orange juice, and a cup of decaf coffee. This omelet truly "rocks"!

YIELD:
SERVES 1 VERY HUNGRY PERSON–OR
SPLIT BETWEEN 2 PEOPLE

INGREDIENTS
PAN-FRIED POTATOES:
18 to 20 small red potatoes
½ cup slivered onions
¼ cup olive oil
¼ teaspoon salt
¼ teaspoon ground black
    pepper
BACON AND EGGS:
8 strips bacon
1 English muffin
3 eggs
¼ teaspoon salt
¼ teaspoon ground black
    pepper
¼ cup whole milk
Extra olive oil, for the pan
3 slices Swiss cheese
TOPPING:
¼ cup chopped fresh parsley
Your favorite hot sauce
(optional)

Directions

Pan-fried potatoes Cut the red potatoes into quarters or eighths, and add to a frying pan with the onions, olive oil, salt, and pepper. Cook over medium to medium-high heat approximately 20 minutes, stirring regularly until the potatoes are browned and tender when stabbed with a fork.

Bacon and eggs In another frying pan, heat 8 slices of bacon until crisp. Toast 1 English muffin. In a mixing bowl, crack 3 eggs, add salt, pepper, and milk, and beat with a whisk. Lightly oil an 8-inch nonstick frying pan, and pour in the egg mixture. Over medium heat, begin cooking the egg. As portions of the egg become cooked, pull it away from the pan and replace the gaps with more liquid egg mixture. You want to achieve a perfectly shaped circle of cooked egg, and by pulling the cooked egg away from the pan, you are also fluffing it up. When there is no more liquid egg, in one half of the pan place 6 strips of chopped cooked bacon (reserve 2 strips for the topping) and torn apart strips of Swiss cheese.

Carefully, using a spatula, fold uncovered egg half toward the cheese and bacon-covered half, forming a half moon shape. If you like your omelet browned, keep cooking for an additional minute.

Toppings Place a dinner plate over the frying pan and flip both over to reveal the perfect omelet! Garnish the omelet and potatoes with fresh parsley, 2 strips of cooked bacon, and your favorite hot sauce (optional).

Caviar Omelet
MARY WILSON OF THE SUPREMES

Years ago in New York City, there was a restaurant that served a great caviar omelet. I never had a recipe for it, but I fondly remember it from my time in the city. One day, I was having lunch with Mary Wilson, and when we started talking about food I mentioned it to her. Without missing a beat, she said, "Now that is a recipe I would like to have to represent me! Here is what I would like on it." And so, this truly Supreme omelet was born!

YIELD:
1 SINGLE DECADENT OMELET

INGREDIENTS

3 eggs

¼ cup milk

¼ teaspoon salt

2 tablespoons olive oil

¼ cup chopped kale

¼ cup sour cream

1 jar (2 oz) caviar (black or red)

3 chopped scallions

⅛ cup chopped chives

⅛ to ¼ additional cup sour cream (for garnish)

1 teaspoon sesame seeds

1 teaspoon red pepper flakes (for garnish)

⅛ cup pea sprouts or radish sprouts (for garnish)

In a small mixing bowl, beat together eggs, milk, and salt. Set aside.

In a small 8-inch frying pan, add olive oil and kale, and turn it up to medium heat. Sauté for 2 minutes, and then remove from the heat. Remove the kale from the pan and set aside, leaving some of the olive oil in the pan.

Add the egg mixture to the frying pan and return to the heated burner. To make a fluffy omelet, use a spatula to constantly draw cooked egg away from the bottom and sides of the pan, encouraging more liquid egg to flow into the spaces. Continue doing this until the egg mixture is quite solid.

Mentally divide the cooking egg into two half-moon shapes, and add the fillings to one side of it only: first comes half of the cooked kale on top of the eggs; followed by the sour cream, distributed across the length of the kale; then add a generous amount of red or black caviar, reserving a small amount of caviar for the top of the omelet. Sprinkle these toppings with half of the scallions and chopped chives.

Carefully, using a spatula, flip the unfilled half of the cooked egg on top of the filled half. Don't be upset if the top layer of eggs rips, since it is going to be facing the bottom once you plate the omelet.

After a minute or so, remove the frying pan from the heat, position your desired dining plate atop of the frying pan, and in a quick motion flip them both upside down at once. Voilà! A perfectly formed and perfectly plated omelet.

Garnish the finished omelet with additional sour cream and the remaining caviar, scallions, and chives. Sprinkle with sesame seeds. Further garnish with the red pepper flakes and the pea or radish sprouts.

Key Lime Coconut Donuts
MARK BEGO

When I saw the pans for these incredible baked donuts, I knew I had to devise a recipe that created donuts that were "rock & roll" worthy. I combined lime with coconut, and—take it from me—these donuts truly are awesome!

INGREDIENTS

1 tablespoon softened butter, to grease

¼ cup white flour, to flour

2 cups white flour

¾ cup white granulated sugar

2 teaspoons baking powder

1 teaspoon salt

¼ teaspoon ground cinnamon

2 beaten eggs

¾ cup whole milk

2 tablespoons melted butter

¼ cup unflavored yogurt

1 tablespoon fresh lime zest

1 tablespoon freshly squeezed lime juice

1 teaspoon vanilla extract

¼ teaspoon lime oil

2 drops green food coloring

FROSTING:

2 cups powdered sugar

¼ teaspoon lime oil

2 drops green food coloring

3 tablespoons whole milk

1 tablespoon lime juice

2 cups shredded sweetened coconut

ADDITIONAL FROSTING:

½ cup powdered sugar

1 tablespoon whole milk

2 drops green food coloring

YIELD:

12 DONUTS

Preheat oven to 350°F, placing a rack in the middle of the oven. Grease 12 donut wells in the donut baking pans with butter and dust with ¼ cup flour.

In one mixing bowl, add the dry ingredients: 2 cups flour, sugar, baking powder, salt, and cinnamon, then whisk.

In a second bowl, mix together the wet ingredients 2 beaten eggs, milk, melted butter, and yogurt. Whisk the liquid until smooth. Add freshly grated lime zest, lime juice, vanilla extract, lime oil, and 1 to 2 drops green food coloring to the liquid ingredients, and mix.

Pour the liquid mixture into the dry mixture, and whisk until you have a smooth and thick batter. Place a large 1-gallon plastic zippered food storage bag (or pastry bag) in a small glass bowl with the opening turned inside out, and fill the bag with batter. Zip the bag shut, or knot it if you are using a pastry bag. With scissors, cut a 1-inch tip off of one of the bottom corners of the bag.

With even and constant pressure, squeeze out batter into each of the 12 donut wells. There is enough batter to make a dozen donuts. Do not over-fill the donut wells, or they will ooze when the batter rises. I used 2 baked donut pans with 6 wells each to accomplish this.

When the donut wells are evenly filled, place the pans in the oven and bake for 10 to 12 minutes. When they are done, they will have risen and will spring back to the touch. The risen tops of the donuts will not brown much, so do not rely on visible browning to estimate doneness.

When the donuts are evenly baked, remove the pans and cool for 5 to 10 minutes. After they have cooled, start to carefully loosen and remove the donuts from the pan. Cool another 5 minutes before frosting.

Frosting: Combine powdered sugar with lime oil, green food coloring, whole milk, and freshly squeezed lime juice. Whisk together.

Hand-dip the molded side of each donut into liquid frosting, giving each of them a generous coating. Place the donuts onto the wire pastry rack to drip. Add approximately 1 tablespoon of sweetened coconut to the top of each donut and slightly press it into the frosting.

Add powdered sugar and whole milk to your measuring cup or mixing bowl that contained the first batch of frosting. Add green food coloring, and whisk together. With the donuts arranged in rows, drizzle lines of darker green frosting over the coconut layer on each donut.

Cherry Pineapple Almond Scones
MARK BEGO

When a friend of mine bought me a pre-made box of scones, I thought to myself, "I bet I can improve on these by making them from scratch." Well, I did it! By adding ingredients I like, such as cherries, pineapple, and almonds, I made what I really think are the best scones on the planet! Don't take my word for it—make these yourself and you'll agree! Along with tea or coffee, these scones are the "bomb"!

YIELD:

16 SCONES

INGREDIENTS

2½ cups flour

½ cup granulated white sugar

1 teaspoon baking powder

¼ teaspoon baking soda

½ teaspoon salt

8 tablespoons (1 large stick) cold butter

½ cup dried cherries

½ cup sugared dried pineapple, cut into little cubes

½ cup sliced almonds

¾ cup sour cream

1 whole egg

2 tablespoons sugar, to sprinkle

1 additional tablespoon flour

TOPPING GLAZE:

2 cups powdered sugar

¼ cup whole milk

GARNISH:

16 dried cherries

48 slivered almonds

Preheat the oven to 400°F, placing a rack in the middle of the oven.

In a large mixing bowl, add the dry ingredients: flour, sugar, baking powder, baking soda, and salt. Using a wire whisk, mix them together.

Using a grater, grate the cold stick of butter into the dry ingredients—or use a knife to cut the butter into small pieces and add to the dry ingredients. Add dried cherries, dried pineapple, and sliced almonds, and stir them into the dry buttery batter.

In a small mixing bowl, place the sour cream and the cracked whole egg, and whisk. Add the sour cream and egg mixture to the dry ingredients, and mix as well. I find that using the wire whisk works great for the first minute or so, but at a certain point, the mixture will be so clumpy that you will need to get into the bowl with your clean hands and knead the dough, making certain to blend in the flour at the bottom of the bowl.

Once you knead the dough into a ball, place on a floured surface and cut in half. Make 2 same-sized balls of dough. Take the first ball of dough and press it out into an 8- or 9-inch-round circle of dough, about 1 inch thick. Pat it together nicely into a smooth wheel. Take 1 tablespoon sugar and sprinkle it on top of your dough wheel. With a sharp knife, cut the scone dough into 8 identical slices, like you would cut a pie. Coat the edges of the triangles of dough with an additional 1 tablespoon flour and remaining 1 tablespoon sugar.

Repeat this process one by one, placing each scone on a cookie sheet covered with parchment paper, to avoid sticking. Repeat the process with the second ball of dough. If there is room, place all 16 triangular scones on the cookie sheet with 1 inch between each to separate. Do not overcrowd them. Baking in two batches of 8 is often easier.

Bake the scones for 15 to 17 minutes in the oven. You want them a nice golden brown on top, but don't burn the bottoms. When they are baked, remove from the oven and let cool for 10 minutes.

Topping glaze: Meanwhile, make the glaze. In a mixing bowl or a large measuring cup, add powdered sugar and milk, and mix together with a wire whisk. If the glaze has a thin texture, add more powdered sugar. You want it thick, but you also want to be able to pour it.

Place the cooled scones on baker's racks over a kitchen counter covered in wax paper. Arrange the scones in one or two rows, like the interlocking teeth of a zipper. Using a measuring cup with a spout, evenly drizzle lines of glaze across the scones. You don't want a full coating of sugar glaze, just tasty strips.

Garnish: While the glaze is still liquid, artistically affix a dried cherry to the top of each scone and a slice of almond at each of the three points. The glaze will set up pretty quick, gluing down the decorative cherry and almonds.

Apple Banana Cranberry Muffins

MARK BEGO

A couple of years ago, I was looking for a muffin recipe that had an ample amount of fruit in it, so the muffins wouldn't be too dense and yet would be healthy and full of flavor. After looking at a couple of recipes that interested me, I developed this one myself. I guarantee that you will love it!

YIELD:
12 REGULAR-SIZED MUFFINS

INGREDIENTS

1 cup whole wheat flour

1 cup all-purpose white flour

½ cup granulated sugar

2 teaspoons baking powder

½ teaspoon baking soda

2 teaspoons cinnamon

1 teaspoon ground cloves

2 tablespoons lemon zest

¼ teaspoon salt

1 cup dried cranberries

1 pared, cored, chopped apple

½ cup chopped or broken pecans

½ cup buttermilk

½ cup vegetable oil

½ cup mashed banana (1 ripe banana)

1 egg

DIRECTIONS

In a large bowl, combine the whole wheat and white flours, sugar, baking powder, baking soda, cinnamon, ground cloves, lemon zest, and salt. Add the dried cranberries, apple, and pecans to the dry ingredients.

In another bowl, mix the buttermilk, vegetable oil, mashed banana, and egg. Mix the liquids into the dry ingredients until blended. *Note:* Do not be alarmed that this is not a batter you can pour. With all of the fruit in it, it will be quite lumpy.

Spoon the chunky batter into 12 greased or paper-lined muffin pan cups. There is so much fruit in these muffins, that the dough will rise minimally, so feel free to mound the fruit and dough batter high in the middle of each muffin.

Bake at 375°F for 20 to 25 minutes for regular-sized muffins. The ultimate test for "doneness" of any muffin is by stabbing the middle of one of them with a toothpick. If you can pull the toothpick out "clean," it is done baking.

Cool the muffins 1 or 2 minutes before removing them from pan. They are absolutely wonderful when they are warm and fresh from the oven!

Crab Cakes Benedict

MARK BEGO

This is by far my favorite breakfast. Although the steps are very detailed, it is easy to achieve impressive and delicious results. And don't worry about making hollandaise sauce from scratch—this amazing recipe shows you how to make the easiest and best hollandaise sauce using a blender. If you do not have a blender, do it by hand with a whisk or hand held mixer.

YIELD:
4 EGGS BENEDICT

INGREDIENTS

CRAB CAKES:
See Crab Cake recipe (page 62)

EGGS AND MUFFINS:
4 eggs
¼ cup vinegar
4 English muffins

HOLLANDAISE SAUCE
½ cup (1 stick) butter
3 egg yolks
½ teaspoon Dijon mustard
1 tablespoon lemon juice

GARNISH:
¼ cup chopped chives
Fresh ground black pepper
Your favorite hot sauce

Make the crab cakes. Keep them warm in an oven preheated to 250°F.

In a large frying pan, add an inch or two of water, and turn it up to medium-high heat. Using a large frying pan to poach the eggs gives you more boiling water surface so the eggs don't stick together. When the water begins to boil, add vinegar (this helps the eggs to stay together). Crack the eggs into the boiling water. Boil for 3 minutes.

Toast English muffins so they are ready when the eggs, the hollandaise, and the crab cakes are done.

Melt the butter. Add egg yolks, mustard, and lemon juice to a blender and blend at medium high speed for 5 or 6 seconds. Slowly pour melted butter into the blender, as you continue to blend. It should only take 1 or 2 minutes to thicken. Set aside. If you use a whisk or hand held mixer, the results are the same—a creamy sauce.

At this point, you should have the crab cakes heated, English muffins toasted, eggs poached, and hollandaise sauce made. Set one or two halves of an English muffin on individual plates, topped with a crab cake, a poached egg, and a generous amount of hollandaise sauce.

Garnish with chopped chives, fresh ground black pepper, and an optional drop or two of your favorite hot sauce.

Lunch, Soups & Salads

"Let's do lunch" is one of my favorite things to hear. And when you sample the recipes in this chapter, you will definitely want to cook up some midday socializing over food. Jimmy Greenspoon of Three Dog Night and Betty Kelly of Martha & The Vandellas share their uniquely different versions of chili (pages 28, 38), while Dennis DeYoung of Styx has a simple way to enliven any salad with his "Fast and Easy" Salad Dressing (page 34). Finally, Mary Wilson's Swordfish Tacos (page 36) are so fresh and crunchy you'll think you are dining seaside!

Credit: George Vissichelli

Credit: MJB Photo Archives

LEFT: This photo of Jimmy Greenspoon and me was taken in 2014 in Chandler, Arizona, where Three Dog Night was headlining at The Ostrich Festival. Although he tragically passed away in 2015, Jimmy always gave 100% of his energy to everything he did throughout his life.

RIGHT: Betty Kelly of Martha & The Vandellas is an absolute doll. Here we are at the 2016 HAL Awards at the Beverly Hills Hotel. The awards raise money for charity and music scholarships, and Betty is one of their most devoted supporters.

Minestrone

Randy Jones of The Village People

"I have been friends with Mark Bego since 1978," says Randy, "when he was the first music industry journalist to interview me and the original Village People. When I was in Arizona with Mark recently, Bego and I cooked up a batch of minestrone soup. It was excellent, and we covered it in Parmesan cheese and ate it for days. Here is the ultimate version of what we cooked up together in Tucson."

Yield:

12 bowls

Ingredients

½ cup olive oil
1 cup chopped onion
1 cup chopped cabbage
1 cup chopped celery
1 cup chopped carrots
⅛ cup chopped garlic
1 cup zucchini, sliced and cut in half
1 cup green beans, cleaned and cut into 1-inch segments
1 can (28 oz) diced tomatoes
2 cans (15 oz each) tomato sauce
1 can (6 oz) tomato paste
1 can (15 oz) white beans or cannellini beans, rinsed and drained
4 cups chicken broth or vegetable broth
1 cup red wine
3 bay leaves
¼ cup chopped basil leaves
1 tablespoon oregano
1 teaspoon salt
1 teaspoon black pepper

1 cup uncooked pasta: either elbows, spirals, or shells are best
1 cup grated Parmesan cheese

1 cup chopped Italian flat-leaf parsley

Directions

In a large, deep cooking pot, add olive oil, onions, cabbage, celery, carrots, garlic, zucchini, and green beans. Sauté them.

When the vegetables are getting tender, add the diced tomatoes, tomato sauce, tomato paste, white or cannellini beans, broth, red wine, bay leaves, basil leaves, oregano, salt, and black pepper. Bring the mixture to a boil, and then simmer at low heat for 30 minutes.

Add the cup of uncooked pasta, and continue to simmer for 12 to 15 minutes, until the pasta is al dente. Remove the bay leaves before serving. Serve the soup in individual bowls, topped with grated Parmesan cheese and chopped Italian flat leaf parsley.

Three Alarm Chili
JIMMY GREENSPOON OF THREE DOG NIGHT

> I asked Jimmy if he thought we should increase the spicy setting and "make adding habanero peppers the 'Three Alarm' setting on the hotness scale." His reply was, "God, no! People will be suing me to have their carpets cleaned if they feed it to their dogs and cats!"

YIELD:

SERVES 4 TO 6 PEOPLE

INGREDIENTS

1 lb ground turkey or
  ground beef
1 oz olive oil
¼ cup olive oil
1 large chopped onion
1 chopped red bell pepper

FOR "ONE ALARM" CHILI, ADD:
2 to 3 tablespoons chili
  powder

FOR "TWO ALARM" CHILI, ADD IN

ADDITION TO THE ABOVE:
2 teaspoons finely
  chopped fresh serrano
  chili pepper

FOR "THREE ALARM" CHILI, ADD

IN ADDITION TO THE ABOVE:
2 teaspoons finely
  chopped fresh jalapeño
  chili pepper

1 can (28 oz) diced
  tomatoes
2 cans (15 oz each)
  tomato sauce
2 teaspoons salt
1 teaspoon black pepper
1 teaspoon garlic powder

1 can (15 oz) black beans, rinsed and drained
1 can (15 oz) red kidney beans, rinsed and drained
OPTIONAL:
16 oz sour cream
2 cups grated Cheddar cheese

DIRECTIONS

In a small frying pan, brown the ground turkey or ground beef. If you are using turkey, add 1 oz olive oil to the pan so it doesn't stick.

In a large, deep cooking pot, add ¼ cup olive oil, onion, red bell pepper, and the chili powder and/or serrano pepper and/or jalapeño pepper, depending on how hot you want your chili to be. Sauté until tender. In the cooking pot, add the diced tomatoes, tomato sauce, salt, pepper, and garlic powder.

Add black beans and red beans to the cooking pot, then add the browned ground turkey or beef. Stir together over medium heat until it comes to a boil. Reduce the heat to low, and continue to simmer for 45 minutes. Stir occasionally. Serve in bowls with a large spoon.

Optional: Top with sour cream and Cheddar cheese. Greenspoon adds, "Instead of using Cheddar cheese, a great substitute is to use a Mexican spiced jack cheese, grated on top."

NOTE: Another tip from Jimmy: "Some people really like corn in chili, as that makes it more 'Southwestern.' If you want, add one can (15 oz) of corn kernels, drained. You could serve this with your favorite tortilla or taco chips, dipping them in the chili."

Macaroni Salad
Jay Siegel of The Tokens

Jay says, "Here is one of my 'standard oldies but delicious goodies!" And indeed, he is correct. What sixties diner would be without macaroni salad on the menu, next to the hot dogs and hamburgers? And, what diner would be without a copy of The Tokens' signature number one 1961 hit, "The Lion Sleeps Tonight"? None that I know of! Jay's macaroni salad recipe is a rock & roll classic, and so is he!

Yield:
Serves 6 to 8 people as a side dish

Ingredients
8 oz elbow macaroni
1 diced tomato
1 cup diced celery
3 tablespoons chopped green pepper
½ cup mayonnaise
1 tablespoon lemon juice
1 teaspoon salt
1 teaspoon sugar
¼ teaspoon celery seed

Directions

Cook the macaroni in boiling water until al dente. Drain and rinse with cold water. In a mixing bowl, add the macaroni, tomato, celery, and green pepper.

In a small bowl, combine the mayonnaise, lemon juice, salt, sugar, and celery seed. Add the flavored mayonnaise to the bowl of macaroni and chopped vegetables. Carefully fold the ingredients together.

Chill in the refrigerator for 1 hour before serving.

Bison Burger on a Bed of Greens

Debbie Gibson

When I asked Debbie what her favorite burger was, she informed me without hesitation that it is a bison burger on a bed of greens. She chose bison "because it's lean—and the flavor!" When I inquired about her favorite bun, she replied, "No bun. On a bed of greens." If you haven't tried it, bison is a very lean meat and a great protein choice. I tried it exactly the way she likes it—on greens—and I loved it. Way to go, Chef Debbie!

Yield:
Serves 3 or 4 people, depending on the size of burgers

Ingredients

1 lb ground bison meat
1 to 2 teaspoons salt, to taste
1 to 2 medium to large onions
¼ cup olive oil
1 oz olive oil
1 lb goat cheese
1 lb fresh arugula
½ cup mayonnaise
1 large-leafed head iceberg lettuce (to make a vegan bun for the burger)
1 or 2 sliced tomatoes
1 sliced avocado

Directions

If the bison meat is frozen, fully defrost it. If the ground bison meat is not already in patties, form it into individual quarter-pound or third-pound burger patties, and season with salt only. Debbie prefers hers in the quarter-pound size.

Cut the onions in half and slice so you have half-moon pieces. In a small frying pan over medium heat, add onions and olive oil. Stirring frequently, sauté the onions until they start to brown. Remove from heat and set aside.

In a cast iron or other heavy frying pan, add an additional 1 oz olive oil and heat to a medium-high temperature. Add the patties to the pan, and sear and cook on both sides. Debbie likes her burger cooked to a beautiful pink interior at a "medium rare" temperature. I, on the other hand, like a more thoroughly done "medium well." Cook however you like it. In the last 3 minutes, add creamy goat cheese to the tops of the patties so that they start to melt.

Add the grilled onions on top and serve with arugula and other toppings. Debbie's list of favorite accompaniments include garnishes like mayonnaise, lettuce, tomato, and avocado.

"Fast and Easy" Salad Dressing
DENNIS DEYOUNG OF STYX

Before I asked Dennis DeYoung, famed lead singer and keyboard player of Styx, for a recipe, I had no idea what a humorous guy he actually is! Styx and their hit song "Mr. Roboto" should have a been a tip-off that Dennis is, indeed, a fun guy. He is also someone who knows what he likes when it comes to food. He has described this recipe, his favorite salad dressing, as being "fast and easy." This is great on an Italian Caprese salad of tomatoes, mozzarella cheese, and fresh basil.

YIELD:
ENOUGH SALAD DRESSING FOR
4 TO 6 SALADS

INGREDIENTS
16 fresh basil leaves
1 cup olive oil
⅓ cup balsamic vinegar
3 tablespoons sugar

NOTE: To make a Caprese salad like the one in the photo, alternate layers of sliced tomatoes, slices of fresh mozzarella cheese, and fresh basil leaves. Add a generous amount of Dennis DeYoung's great salad dressing.

Chop the basil leaves and put them in a small mixing bowl. "Four leaves cut up per serving. I like a lot of basil!" says Dennis. "I rip the leaves with my fingers 'cause I play keyboards and have grown fond of my fingers. My reluctance with knives has kept me out of contention for the annual Wolfgang Puck Award for best self-promotion."

Add olive oil to the mixing bowl. Dennis prefers Bertolli light olive oil. As Dennis says, "I know everyone says use extra virgin as if it cures all disease and financial problems, but I think for salad, 'light' tastes better."

Next, add balsamic vinegar to the bowl. "Chef" DeYoung likes Liguria or Colavita balsamic vinegar, but also says, "Use whichever one you prefer." If you want a more vinegary taste, you can certainly add more, says the Styx star. "The standard ratio is three-to-one oil-to-vinegar, but go ahead, buck the system, be a rebel, let your freak flag fly, do it to taste."

Add sugar to the bowl. Dennis suggests using sugar that is "preferably organic, nonpesticidal, non-GMO-dal, nonsteroidal, non-PED-dal, and, most important: non-sequitur-dal." "Actually," he adds, "the stuff you put in your coffee will be fine, even if it's some awful sugar substitute, which should be renamed 'Icky Poo.'"

Dennis instructs, "Pour all the ingredients of this witches' brew into a glass, bowl, cup, or ten-gallon hat, then stir vigorously until the sugar, basil, oil, and vinegar meld into a thicker concoction." A wire whisk is perfect for this.

Now it is time to taste your favorite salad. Or, as Dennis says, "Pour the nectar over your salad, whatever it is (unless it's kale, yuck) and enjoy! Remember: if you try this dressing and don't care for it, next year you will be audited by the IRS! Cheers, Dennis."

Swordfish Tacos

MARY WILSON OF THE SUPREMES

Fish tacos have been a staple in beach resorts for years, but you don't have to travel to the seaside to enjoy this recipe. Mary says, "I prefer a denser fish like swordfish for tacos, but cod will certainly work too. You can fry the tortillas for crunchy shells, or leave them uncooked for a soft taco."

YIELD:

12 TACOS, SERVES
4 TO 6 PEOPLE

INGREDIENTS

1 lb swordfish or cod
1 teaspoon turmeric
1 teaspoon powdered garlic
¼ teaspoon salt
¼ teaspoon pepper
12 corn tortillas
¼ to ½ cup olive oil (optional, for crunchy tacos)
1 thinly sliced cucumber
1 cup slivered carrots
1 slivered red bell pepper
1 thinly sliced avocado
2 cups shredded red or green cabbage

OPTIONAL:

Serve with your favorite hot sauce or salsa

DIRECTIONS

Cut the fish into 1-inch slivers, and season with turmeric, garlic, salt, and pepper. For an even coating, dust the fish with the spices using a fine sieve.

If you want your tortillas to be soft, skip this step. If you want your tacos crunchy, add olive oil to a frying pan over medium to medium-high heat. Using kitchen tongs, individually fry the corn tortillas on both sides until lightly browned. Halfway into frying them, use the tongs to fold them in half so that they are ready to be stuffed. As they reach the desired crunchiness, remove from the pan and place on a plate lined with paper towels to absorb excess oil.

To cook the fish, you have the option of either baking or broiling it. To bake: preheat the oven to 350°F, and place the fish in a tempered glass or metal baking dish that has a light coating of olive oil. Bake the fish for 7 to 10 minutes. To broil: set oven to "broil," place the fish in a metal baking dish, and place in the oven for 5 to 7 minutes, turning it over halfway.

You are ready to assemble the tacos. Add the cooked fish to the taco shells, and layer with cucumber, carrots, red pepper, avocado, and cabbage. Top with your favorite hot sauce or salsa as desired.

Crock-Pot Chili
Betty Kelly of Martha & The Vandellas

Betty Kelly gave me her recipe for Crock-Pot Chili when we were both at a gathering of The Heroes and Legends Awards cocktail party in Los Angeles. "This chili is so easy to make, and I just love it," she says. This quick homemade chili can be made in an electric slow cooker; it can also be simmered and covered on the stove. With Italian-style tomatoes, Mexican-style salsa, and Betty's own Motown flair, it is so packed with flavor that there is literally "Nowhere to Run" from it!

YIELD:

SERVES 4 TO 6 PEOPLE

INGREDIENTS
1 lb ground beef
1 can (15.5 oz) red kidney beans
1 can (28 oz) Italian-style diced tomatoes
1 cup Mexican-style tomato salsa
1 tablespoon sugar
1 packet (1.25 oz) chili spice mix*

I took it upon myself to take Betty's chili spice mix and break it down into a create-it-yourself spice mix.

* Substitute chili spice mix with the following:
1 tablespoon flour
1½ teaspoons chili powder
½ teaspoon salt
½ teaspoon oregano
½ teaspoon cumin
½ teaspoon garlic powder
½ teaspoon onion powder
½ teaspoon ground black pepper

DIRECTIONS

In a frying pan, brown the ground beef and drain off fat and juices. Rinse and drain the kidney beans. In a slow cooker or Crock-Pot, combine the cooked ground beef, kidney beans, diced tomatoes, salsa, sugar, and spice mix. Stir the ingredients together.

If you plan to eat this soon, set the slow cooker's temperature at high heat, and let it cook for 1½ hours. If you are able to make this an all-day simmering dish while you are away, set the slow cooker temperature at the lowest temperature, and cook for 4 up to 8 hours. If you want to use a conventional stove, bring the mixture to a boil and lower the setting from medium-high to low heat. Cook for 45 minutes to 1 hour.

NOTE: This hearty and spicy chili can be garnished with sour cream, raw onions, and shredded Cheddar cheese.

Tomato Artichoke Soup
Mary Wilson & Mark Bego

At a great Italian restaurant in Louisville during the 2014 Kentucky Derby, Mary Wilson and I fell in love with their tomato and artichoke soup. Instead of asking the restaurant for their recipe, we simply took note of what appeared to be in it and proceeded to give the artichoke soup our own "spin," kicking up the flavors by adding half-and-half, garlic, onions, oregano, basil, and olive oil. When I said, "I think you would start with a large can of chopped tomatoes," Mary, who had just told me how great tomatoes are for your health, rolled her eyes and said, "Canned tomatoes? I think you should use fresh chopped tomatoes." To give credence to both methods, this recipe gives you the choice: freshly chopped or canned.

Yield:
Enough soup for
4 to 6 people

Ingredients
2 cups chopped onion
2 cups chopped celery
½ cup chopped garlic
¼ cup olive oil
¼ cup fresh chopped oregano
¼ cup fresh chopped basil
1 can (28 oz) diced tomatoes or 3½ cups freshly diced tomatoes
1 can (15 oz) tomato sauce
1 pint half-and-half (or 1 cup heavy cream and 1 cup whole milk)
1 cup white wine
1 can (14 oz) quartered artichoke hearts
2 teaspoons salt
1 teaspoon ground black pepper
1 cup grated Parmesan cheese

Directions

In a large pot, combine the onions, celery, garlic, and olive oil. Sauté the vegetables over medium high heat, until slightly softened.

Add the oregano, basil, canned or fresh tomatoes, tomato sauce, half-and-half, white wine, artichoke hearts, salt, and pepper to the pot. Stir together and bring to a boil.

When the soup begins to bubble, turn down to a low temperature and continue to simmer for 30 minutes. The flavors will begin to meld together, and the creamy half-and-half takes on the red color and taste of the tomatoes. Stir occasionally to avoid burning the vegetables at the bottom.

Serve the soup in individual bowls, sprinkling with Parmesan cheese.

Vegan Caviar Black Bean Salad

Mark Bego

I call this *caviar* simply because just about everything in it is corn kernel-sized, and because it can be eaten on a cracker. The first time I had this innovative salad, I was surprised that it packed so much flavor. This is the perfect dish to prepare as a vegetarian or vegan option during a lunch or barbecue. Serve as a lunch-sized salad on Boston lettuce or arugula, or as a colorful side dish to complement a sandwich or a burger.

Yield:
Serves 12 to 16 people as a side dish

Ingredients
1 can (14 oz) black beans
1 can (14 oz) corn kernels
1 can (14 oz) garbanzo beans
1 chopped red bell pepper
1 cup chopped fresh purple onion
1 cup chopped cherry tomatoes
½ cup chopped fresh cilantro
6 chopped scallions (both green and white parts)
2 teaspoons ground cumin
1 teaspoon dried or freshly chopped oregano
¼ cup rice wine vinegar
½ cup olive oil
¼ cup freshly squeezed lemon juice
1 teaspoon sea salt
1 teaspoon ground black pepper

Directions

Drain and rinse the black beans, corn, and garbanzo beans. Place in a large mixing bowl, along with red bell pepper, onion, tomatoes, cilantro, and scallions. Add the cumin, oregano, rice wine vinegar, olive oil, lemon juice, salt and pepper. Gently mix together.

Place the mixture in the refrigerator for 1 hour. You should stir the mixture a couple of times through, to make sure the beans and vegetables marinate in the dressing and are full of flavor. Remove from refrigerator and serve chilled.

Detroit-Style Coney Dogs
MARK BEGO

Being from Detroit and being a true Motown boy, this classic recipe is pure Motor City to me! After years of eating Coney dogs in Detroit, I can tell you that this recipe for Coney dog sauce, which I came up with, is "the real deal"!

YIELD:
8 TO 12 CONEY DOGS

INGREDIENTS

DETROIT-STYLE CONEY DOG SAUCE:
¼ cup olive oil
1 cup chopped white onion
1 lb ground beef
¼ cup water
1 can (15 oz) tomato sauce
2 tablespoons prepared yellow
   mustard
1 tablespoon celery seed
1½ teaspoons chili powder
1 teaspoon garlic powder
1 teaspoon paprika
1 teaspoon ground cumin
1 teaspoon salt
1 teaspoon onion powder
⅛ teaspoon cayenne pepper
   (red pepper)

HOT DOGS:
8 to 12 hot dogs
8 to 12 hot dog buns

GARNISH:
1 cup chopped white onions
1 bottle (8 oz) prepared yellow
   mustard

In a frying pan, add the olive oil. Add the onions and sauté until softened. Add the ground beef and brown the meat, while mixing in the onions.

When the onion-flavored beef is browned, add water and tomato sauce, and stir. Add prepared yellow mustard and all of the spices: celery seed, chili powder, garlic powder, paprika, ground cumin, salt, onion powder, and cayenne pepper. Simmer this meaty, red Coney dog sauce for 45 minutes over medium low heat, until it thickens and all of the flavors meld together.

Grill, pan-fry, or boil the hot dogs. When the Coney dog sauce and hot dogs are ready to serve, place an opened hot dog bun on a plate and top with a cooked hot dog. I like to add a generous amount of Detroit-Style Coney Dog Sauce on the dog and bun.

Finally, garnish it with chopped onions and an additional squirt of prepared yellow mustard. Although it will be slightly sloppy, you should still be able to pick it up to eat it.

Lobster & Shrimp Salad Sandwich

MARK BEGO

When I was working at one of my first jobs in the publishing business in New York City, my boss, Alyse Dorese, would occasionally send me out to get us lunch. I will always remember the sandwiches I would get at a local midtown deli: shrimp salad on a Kaiser roll. Fast forward to the present: recently, I opened up my freezer at lunchtime and found not only shrimp but also lobster tail–and I instantly knew what I had to do! This sandwich not only brought back my NYC lunch memories, it also improved upon them.

YIELD:
1 DECADENTLY OVERSTUFFED SANDWICH OR 2 SMALLER SANDWICHES

INGREDIENTS
1 lobster tail
5 large raw shrimp
¼ cup olive oil
½ cup mayonnaise
¼ cup chopped onion
¼ cup chopped celery
½ teaspoon ground black pepper
1 teaspoon dried dill weed
1 Kaiser roll

GARNISH:
1 cup chopped iceberg lettuce, arugula, or other greens

DIRECTIONS

If you are using frozen lobster tail and shrimp, place them in lukewarm water to defrost. Using kitchen scissors, slit the lobster tail in half from tail tip to thick end. Leave the shell intact. You can either remove the shells from the shrimp or cook them intact and peel after cooking.

In a cast iron or other heavy frying pan over medium-high heat, add the olive oil. When the oil is hot, place the lobster tails in the pan, meat side down. When it starts to cook, add the shrimp to the pan. You may have to turn the lobster several times until the meat is cooked and the outer shell is bright red. It shouldn't take any more than 5 to 7 minutes to cook the shrimp and lobster. Remove from the heat, and allow the shrimp and lobster to cool.

When cool, remove the meat from the shells and cut it into small pieces. In a mixing bowl, add the lobster, shrimp, mayonnaise, onion, celery, black pepper, and dill weed, and mix together.

Slice the Kaiser roll horizontally, and assemble the sandwich. Garnish with iceberg lettuce, arugula, or other greens.

Hors D'Oeuvres

Whether you are creating hors d'oeuvres for a party or appetizers for a dinner, you want them to be not only delicious but also visually appealing. Randy Jones of The Village People presents a new spin on an Italian classic with his Caprese Bruschetta with Prosciutto (page 58), Joey Fatone's Rice Balls (page 50) deliver exciting flavor and crunch, and Mary Wilson's Grilled Artichokes & Dipping Sauce (page 60) are elegant and fun to eat.

Credit: Derek Storm   Credit: MJB Photo Archives

LEFT: Randy Jones and I have been close friends since the 1970s, and we have cooked up all sorts of projects together, as well as some great food, too. Here we are at my birthday party in 2005 at The Cutting Room in New York City.
RIGHT: Joey Fatone, Mary Wilson, and I at Churchill Downs in Louisville for the most exciting horse race in the world, the Kentucky Derby.

Rice Balls
JOEY FATONE OF 'N SYNC

Joey Fatone is someone Mary Wilson and I know from the Kentucky Derby and the annual Barnstable Brown Gala in Louisville. Joey is a great guy to run into, and he always seems to be the life of any party he attends. Here, "Chef" Fatone shares his recipe for one of his favorite things to make as a perfect party snack.

YIELD:

MAKES 24 RICE BALLS

INGREDIENTS

2 eggs
⅓ cup grated Parmesan cheese
1 tablespoon dried parsley
¼ teaspoon freshly ground black pepper
1 teaspoon salt
2 cups water
1 teaspoon salt
1 cup uncooked white rice
1½ cups dried breadcrumbs
2 cups olive oil

DIRECTIONS

In a medium bowl, whisk together the eggs, cheese, parsley, pepper, and 1 teaspoon salt. Cover and refrigerate.

In a large saucepan, pour in water and 1 teaspoon salt, and bring to a boil. Stir in the rice, cover, and reduce heat to the lowest temperature. Cook rice for 20 minutes until water is almost absorbed, stirring frequently. Remove from heat.

Slowly pour the egg mixture into the saucepan, stirring rapidly as you pour to prevent the egg from scrambling. Allow rice mixture to cool for one hour.

Pour breadcrumbs into a pile on one end of a cutting board. Dampen hands and roll rice mixture into 1-inch balls. Then coat each one with breadcrumbs.

In a small, deep skillet, heat olive oil to 350°F (make sure oil covers the rice balls). Fry rice balls, six at a time, turning as needed to ensure even browning. Drain on paper towels and serve warm.

NOTE: These are ideal as an hors d'oeuvre, as a side course to an Italian meal, or for a party buffet table. They can be eaten alone, or dipped in marinara sauce or barbecue sauce. They also keep fully cooked in the refrigerator in a zippered storage bag for up to 2 days, and are easily reheated in a preheated 350°F oven for 15 minutes. To quote Mr. Fatone when he gave me this recipe: "Enjoy!"

Baked Artichoke Dip
SPANKY McFARLANE OF SPANKY & OUR GANG

"This is a recipe I love!" Spanky says. "I was at a party, and someone had made this incredible dip that was made of artichoke hearts, baked in the oven with Parmesan cheese. You can spread it on little rounds of bread or crackers, and it is out of this world!" I remember first seeing Spanky McFarlane on TV's *The Ed Sullivan Show* in the 1960s when the band's "I'd Like to Get to Know You" was a huge Top Ten smash. There was Spanky, go-go-ing in her mini skirt and singing her heart out with her clear and ultra-strong voice. I met her in Santa Monica recently, and she was enthusiastic about contributing a recipe. Although she didn't have a written-down recipe, she described the food so perfectly that it wasn't long before I got the measurements right on target.

YIELD:
SERVES A PARTY OF 12 TO 18 PEOPLE

INGREDIENTS
1 package (8 oz) cream cheese
2 cups of mayonnaise
2 cups grated Parmesan cheese
2 teaspoons cayenne (red) pepper
2 teaspoons garlic powder
2 cans (14 oz each) quartered artichoke hearts

TO SERVE:
Crackers, chips, or sliced bread

DIRECTIONS

In a large mixing bowl, cream together all ingredients except the artichoke hearts. When you have a smooth mixture, add the artichoke hearts and fold into the creamy, cheesy sauce.

Spoon the mixture into a baking dish or several smaller baking dishes. Preheat the oven to 350°F, and bake the dip for 25 to 30 minutes. When it is done, it will be bubbling around the edges and show the beginnings of browning on the outer surface. Remove from the oven, and serve hot.

NOTE: Most baking dishes list how many cups they hold. This recipe creates 2 cups of artichoke dip, so you can plan what baking dish to select.

Empanadas
Cory Daye of Dr. Buzzard's Original Savannah Band

The lovely Ms. Daye proclaims, "Although I'm now a vegetarian, this is a recipe from my Latin roots, when I ate meat: *Dios mio!*"

Yield:
Approximately 48 empanadas

Ingredients

Dough:

8 oz softened cream cheese
("My secret ingredient!")
½ cup butter or margarine
1½ cups all-purpose flour
⅛ teaspoon salt

Meat filling:

1 tablespoon olive oil
2 tablespoons minced onion
2 crushed cloves of garlic
½ lb lean ground beef
¼ cup crushed and drained
tomatoes
2 tablespoons chopped
pimiento-stuffed olives
½ teaspoon oregano leaves
1 tablespoon capers (optional)
1 tablespoon minced green
pepper
1 tablespoon Bijol*
1 tablespoon recaíto**
Salt and pepper, to taste
1 egg yolk
1 tablespoon water

In a large mixing bowl, blend cream cheese and butter with a hand mixer. Gradually add flour and salt. Blend until dough is smooth, and knead it by hand until consistent. Divide dough into 3 balls and chill in refrigerator for 30 minutes.

Heat olive oil in a medium skillet, and sauté the onions and garlic until transparent. Add the beef and stir until browned, about 5 minutes. Stir in tomatoes, olives, oregano, capers (optional), green pepper, Bijol, recaíto, salt, and pepper. Simmer uncovered for about 5 minutes, stirring occasionally. Drain the mixture if there's too much liquid.

Preheat oven to 400°F. On a lightly floured surface, roll each ball of dough one at a time to ⅛-inch thickness. Using a biscuit cutter with a 3-inch diameter or a drinking glass with the same measurement (as Cory says, "Bronx style!"), cut out circles in the dough. Spoon about 1 teaspoon of meat mixture onto one side of each circle.

For the next step, Cory advises: "Have a small bowl of water on hand to moisten the edges of the empanadas." Fold pastry over the filling to form a half-moon shape, moisten edges with water, and press edges to seal. Crimp with fork tines. Prick the top of the empanadas with a toothpick to allow steam to escape.

Mix egg yolk with 1 tablespoon of water and brush over the surface of the empanadas. Place on cookie sheets and bake until golden (about 12 to 15 minutes).

* "Bijol is a seasoning condiment and is optional if you can't find a bodega near you . . . ha ha ha!" says Cory.
** "You can find recaíto (frozen or jarred) in the Goya section of your grocery store." Since recaíto is cilantro paste, you can also substitute it with dried cilantro flakes.

Thick or Thin Crust Pizza
WALTER EGAN

Walter says, "I am very much a traditionalist when it comes to pizza. Tomato sauce, mozzarella cheese, and Parmesan cheese is all I like on mine."

YIELD:
2 THIN CRUST PIZZAS OR
1 THICK CRUST PIZZA

INGREDIENTS

CRUST:
- 2¾ cups flour (plus extra for dusting)
- 1 tablespoon salt
- 1 cup warm water (100 to 110°F)
- ¼ oz active dry yeast
- 1½ teaspoons sugar
- 2 tablespoons olive oil (plus extra for greasing)
- ¼ cup of cornmeal

SAUCE:
- 1 can (15 oz) tomato sauce
- 1 teaspoon garlic powder
- 1 teaspoon oregano
- ½ teaspoon salt

TOPPINGS:
- 2 cups shredded mozzarella cheese
- ¼ cup of grated Parmesan cheese

OPTIONAL TOPPINGS:
- 18 pieces sliced pepperoni
- ¼ cup chopped onions
- ¼ cup chopped green pepper

In a large mixing bowl, combine the flour and salt for the crust. Create a well in the center of the flour and salt mixture, and pour the water into the well. Sprinkle in the yeast and the sugar. Let stand for 5 to 10 minutes, until it bubbles.

Pour in the olive oil. Stir the mixture together to create a rough dough. Remove the dough from the bowl, and place on a surface dusted with flour. Knead the dough for 1 or 2 minutes until spongy and uniform. Grease the surface of the mixing bowl, return the dough to it, and cover the bowl with a damp cloth kitchen towel or paper towels. Let the dough sit in a warm place for 2 hours until it doubles in size.

Meanwhile, in a small saucepan, add the tomato sauce, garlic powder, oregano and salt. Heat to medium-high heat, and then remove from the stove to cool and set aside.

Preheat the oven to 450°F. After the dough has risen, place a ceramic pizza stone (or baking sheet) in the oven to preheat. Sprinkle the surface of a cutting board or pizza peel (large wooden pizza spatula) with cornmeal. With a rolling pin or by hand, carefully stretch out the dough to form a 14-inch-round pizza crust. If you are making 2 thin crust pizzas, divide the pizza dough into 2 halves.

Spread the pizza sauce across the crust, leaving the outer inch empty around the circumference. If you are adding the optional toppings of pepperoni, onions, and green peppers, evenly distribute them on top of the pizza sauce. Top the pizza with mozzarella and Parmesan cheese.

Remove the preheated pizza stone (or baking sheet) from the oven. Carefully place the pizza onto the pizza stone by sliding it off the cutting board or pizza peel. Bake the pizza in the oven for 10 to 15 minutes for thin crust, or 15 to 20 minutes for thick crust. Slice with a pizza wheel, and prepare to enjoy one incredible treat!

Caprese Bruschetta with Prosciutto

RANDY JONES OF THE VILLAGE PEOPLE

The Village People's original "Cowboy," Randy Jones, says, "Whenever I give a party, this is my favorite hors d'oeuvre to make." These easy-to-make mini open-face sandwiches, with their layers of Italian flavors, are great appetizers for any party. Speaking of parties, I remember going to some truly wild events at Randy's massive loft in Greenwich Village back in the 1980s. Oh well, that is a whole other story, and it has nothing to do with these delicious appetizers!

YIELD:

APPROXIMATELY 24 APPETIZERS

INGREDIENTS
1 long loaf Italian bread
¼ cup olive oil
6 to 8 Italian plum tomatoes
8 oz sliced mozzarella cheese
3 oz prosciutto

OPTIONAL:
24 fresh basil leaves
Colored toothpicks or party picks to hold sandwiches together

DIRECTIONS

Preheat the oven to 350°F. Slice the Italian bread into approximately 24 individual slices. Pour olive oil into a shallow bowl, and dip the bread slices one by one in the oil. Arrange the slices of bread, oiled side up, onto a baking sheet. Place in the oven for 10 minutes, or until the bread begins to brown around the edges and the tops.

Remove from the oven. Slice the tomatoes to make 24 slices. Cut the sliced cheese into 24 pieces that will comfortably fit on the toasted bread. Slice the prosciutto into 24 pieces. Arrange your appetizers with the bread first, then cheese, followed by a tomato slice, and finally prosciutto (or vice versa). If you would like, add a slice of basil leaf between the tomatoes and prosciutto. You can use your favorite colorful party picks to hold these open-faced sandwiches together.

Grilled Artichokes & Dipping Sauce
MARY WILSON OF THE SUPREMES

According to the Supreme Mary Wilson, "This is a great way to start any meal!"

YIELD:
4 ARTICHOKE HALVES,
TO SERVE 4 PEOPLE

INGREDIENTS
2 large fresh artichokes
½ lemon, juiced
8 tablespoons (1 stick)
  butter
2 tablespoons olive oil
1 tablespoon garlic powder
  or fresh minced garlic
1 tablespoon lemon juice
½ teaspoon cayenne
  pepper
¼ teaspoon salt
Olive oil, to drizzle
(optional)

Trim the tips of the exposed leaves and stems of the artichokes with kitchen scissors. Using a serrated bread knife, slice off the top of the artichoke, 1 inch from the top. Cut the artichoke in half from top to bottom. Squeeze lemon juice on exposed parts of the artichoke or the exposed flesh will quickly turn brown. Using a sharp knife, carefully cut the fuzzy center filaments loose from the interior of the heart. Using a teaspoon, scoop the filaments out, again squeezing lemon juice on the exposed flesh.

According to Mary, place the cleaned artichokes in a large pot of boiling water for 15 to 20 minutes or until tender. Another way to cook them is to steam them (if you are going to grill the artichokes, I recommend using this method, as it adds less water to them and the artichokes stay greener). In a very large pot, place a steamer screen and enough water to come just over the top of the screen. Boil the water on medium-high heat, then turn down to simmer with the lid on. Steam the artichokes for 45 minutes to 1 hour.

To make Mary's dipping sauce, add butter in a small pot and melt it over low heat. Add olive oil, garlic powder, lemon juice, cayenne pepper, and salt. Stir together, and keep warm.

If you steamed the artichokes earlier, I like to add an additional but optional step of grilling the artichokes. Remove them from the steamer pan, and drizzle them with additional olive oil. Using a hot grill pan, singe them on each side for 5 to 8 minutes to give them blackened "grill marks."

To eat the artichokes, remove the leaves one-by-one, dip the meaty tip into small individual bowls of butter sauce, and pull the meat off the bottom of the leaves with your teeth. When you get down to the center of the vegetable, discard any small or thorny inner leaves, cut the heart of the artichoke, and dip pieces of the heart into the butter sauce.

Crab Cakes
MARK BEGO

These crab cakes can be eaten alone as mini appetizers, in a bun as crab burgers, or in a crab cake eggs Benedict. Serve with homemade tartar sauce for dipping or as a topping.

YIELD:

4 MEDIUM-SIZED CRAB CAKES, 3 LARGE CRAB CAKES FOR HAMBURGER BUNS, OR 12 MINI CRAB CAKE HORS D'OEUVRES

INGREDIENTS
8 oz shredded fresh crabmeat
¼ cup breadcrumbs
1 egg
2 tablespoons mayonnaise
1 chopped scallion (both white and green parts)
½ teaspoon salt
½ teaspoon ground black pepper
¼ cup olive oil or vegetable oil
¼ cup additional breadcrumbs

TARTAR SAUCE:
⅓ cup mayonnaise
3 tablespoons pickle relish or chopped pickled cucumber
1 tablespoon capers
1 teaspoon dill weed

DIRECTIONS

In a mixing bowl, combine the crabmeat, breadcrumbs, egg, mayonnaise, chopped scallion, salt, and pepper, and mix well. Place oil (add more if needed) in a frying pan over medium to medium-high heat.

Pour additional breadcrumbs in a bowl or small plate. Divide the mixture in the bowl into quarters or thirds. Using your clean hands, form the mixture into crab patties. The mixture is dense enough to hold together in your hands, but to add more support and an extra bit of texture, place the burger-shaped crab patty in the additional breadcrumbs. Evenly coat the tops and bottoms.

When the oil is heated, place crab cakes in the frying pan and cook until nicely brown on both sides. Cooking time will vary a bit depending on the heat of your pan. Usually 4 minutes per side works perfectly for me. When you are finished, they should be brown and crispy on both sides.

To make your own tartar sauce, mix together mayonnaise and pickle relish or your own chopped pickles. I love adding capers and dill weed to it, as well.

Deep Fried Tofu

MARK BEGO

I first had these delicious vegetarian appetizers in a Japanese restaurant and instantly fell in love. If you even remotely think that you don't like dishes with tofu, this might just change your opinion. Using extra-firm tofu is the secret to creating cooked tofu that isn't mushy. With the tasty crunch of panko breadcrumbs, the zest of freshly chopped scallions, and the nice salty bite of either soy sauce or ponzu sauce, this recipe is a yummy winner that will convert even tofu-haters!

YIELD:

12 PIECES

INGREDIENTS
1 brick (14 oz) extra-firm
   tofu
2 cups panko breadcrumbs
1 teaspoon ground ginger
   (or 1 teaspoon Chinese
   five spice)
1 cup flour
2 beaten eggs

GARNISH:
6 to 8 freshly sliced
   scallions
1¼ to 1½ cup soy sauce or
   ponzu sauce

EQUIPMENT:
A home deep fryer is the
   best way to do this. If
   you are well versed in
   deep frying on the stove
   top, that works, too.

Drain liquid from the tofu. Cut the tofu in half lengthwise, and then cut each stick of tofu into 6 pieces, 1 inch thick. Heat the deep fryer to 375°F. While it warms up, place the panko breadcrumbs in a small bowl or dish, and add either ground ginger or Chinese five spice to the breadcrumbs.

Dredge tofu slices one by one in the flour, making all six sides relatively dry. Skewer the slices with a bamboo skewer (or a fork) and dip into the beaten egg. When the entire tofu slice is covered in egg wash, place into the bowl of spiced panko breadcrumbs. Make certain to get breadcrumbs stuck to all sides of the tofu by using a spoon to press breadcrumbs into the tofu.

Using the bamboo skewer, place the breaded tofu, standing upright, into the deep fryer basket (note: do not place the basket into the hot oil until all tofu slices are in). Carefully remove the skewer by holding the tofu cube down and pulling away the skewer. Make sure none of the tofu slices are touching each other in the deep fryer basket. If you must, fry them in batches.

Place the basket into the hot oil, and deep fry for 3 to 5 minutes. You want a nicely browned and crunchy deep-fried effect. When the tofu cubes are done, place them upright on a flat plate, garnish with scallions and serve with soy sauce or ponzu sauce.

NOTE: Bamboo shish kebab skewers will come in handy when making these, or a well-placed fork. Use them to skewer and completely coat the tofu cubes without having to touch them with your hands and damage their pre-fried coating.

Sesame Chicken Stuffed Endive

MARK BEGO

YIELD:

24 TO 36 INDIVIDUAL PIECES

INGREDIENTS

4 cups skinless chicken
breast meat (about 3 to
4 breasts)

2 tablespoons olive oil

5 to 6 heads endive
lettuce

3 tablespoons organic
peanut butter

1 tablespoon hoisin sauce

2 to 3 tablespoons
Chinese hot chili oil

2 tablespoons soy sauce

2 tablespoons sesame oil

3 tablespoons vegetable
broth (use vegetable
bouillon cubes or
concentrate)

2 tablespoons rice vinegar

1 tablespoon whole
sesame seeds, plus extra
to garnish

3 to 4 stalks neatly
chopped scallions

Preheat the oven to 350°F. Place the skinless boneless chicken breasts on a baking sheet or heat-resistant baking pan. Drizzle olive oil on the chicken breasts so they don't burn on top or stick to the bottom. Bake for 45 minutes to 1 hour until done. While the chicken is baking, cut ¼ inch off the bottom of the endive heads, and place the exposed stem ends into a bowl of water. Like any other cut plant, it will begin to absorb water. This will give you crispier endive leaves when you stuff them. When the chicken breasts are thoroughly cooked in the middle, remove from the oven and let cool. Cut the meat in 2-inch strips, and shred by hand, following the grain of the meat.

In a saucepan, combine the wet ingredients: the peanut butter, hoisin sauce, hot chili oil, soy sauce, sesame oil, vegetable broth, rice vinegar, and sesame seeds. Over medium heat, continue stirring the ingredients until the oil and liquid ingredients meld together, and the peanut butter melts, about 3 minutes.

In a large mixing bowl, pour the sauce on top of the shredded chicken breasts, and mix together until all of the meat is coated with the sauce. Refrigerate to cool. Take the endive heads out of the water and cut enough of the bottom of the stem off so that the individual leaves come off the bud without you having to tear them loose. You will end up with a nicely shaped "boat" to fill with chicken. Work your way up the stem, freeing more leaves as you slice off more of the stem. You may notice that the leaves get smaller as you go up, but this is not a problem—some people like their hors d'oeuvres big and some like them bite-sized!

Stuff the endive leaves with the chicken mixture, using a fork for uniformity. Garnish with chopped scallions. Sprinkle additional sesame seeds on top of each one. Refrigerate for 1 hour before serving.

Bourbon Meatballs

Mark Bego

This is a recipe I have made for several years. I guarantee that you will not have any leftovers if you make these meatballs for a party. What is my secret to success? Well, really tasty meatballs are a good start, but the key to this delicious appetizer is my totally booze-infused sauce!

Yield:
Approximately 72 meatballs

Ingredients

Meatballs:
1 lb ground beef
1 lb ground turkey, pork, or chicken; or 2 lb beef
2 eggs
1 cup breadcrumbs
⅓ cup Parmesan cheese
1 teaspoon chopped or dried oregano
1 chopped garlic clove
½ cup finely chopped onion
1 teaspoon chopped basil
½ teaspoon salt
½ teaspoon pepper

Bourbon sauce:
2 bottles (18 oz each) barbecue sauce
1 can (6 oz) tomato paste
2 jars (18 oz each) apricot preserves
Tabasco or other hot sauce, to taste (5 to 8 drops are a good start)
1 cup bourbon (Jack Daniels or Southern Comfort are great)

Directions

Meatballs: Preheat the oven to 350°F. Mix all of the meatball ingredients together by hand. Form the mixture into bite-sized balls, about 1½ inches in diameter. For uniformity, use a tablespoon to measure the amount of the meat mixture you use for each ball.

On a large Pyrex baking pan or metal cookie sheet, bake the meatballs for 30 minutes. Remove the meatballs from the oven. Use cooking tongs or a spatula to loosen them from the bottom of the pan if they are stuck.

Bourbon sauce: In a large pan, heat all of the sauce ingredients, except the bourbon, stirring constantly. Bring to a boil, then stir in the Jack Daniels or Southern Comfort bourbon. Add the cooked meatballs.

Keep warm in a chafing dish. Serve with toothpicks or a slotted or regular serving spoon as hors d'oeuvres.

NOTE: You can also use these great meatballs in spaghetti sauce as well, on top of pasta.

68 · Bourbon Meatballs

Coconut Shrimp

Mark Bego

You can serve these as appetizers or a main course.

Yield:
24 to 30 shrimp

Ingredients

Orange dipping sauce:
1 cup orange marmalade
3 tablespoons apple cider vinegar
1 teaspoon red chili pepper flakes

Shrimp and coating:
⅓ cup flour
1 teaspoon salt
1 teaspoon ground black pepper
1 cup sweetened shredded coconut
⅔ cup panko breadcrumbs
2 eggs
1 lb deveined and shelled shrimp, leaving tails on (about 30 medium-sized shrimp)

Equipment:
A home deep fryer is the best way to do this. Deep frying on the stove top would work, too. A pair of kitchen tongs also comes in handy for shrimp handling.

In a small bowl, combine orange marmalade with apple cider vinegar and red chili pepper flakes. Mix, and set aside.

Mix the flour, salt, and pepper together in a small bowl. In another small bowl, mix the coconut and panko breadcrumbs. In a third bowl, beat the two eggs with a whisk or a fork. Start heating the frying oil to 375°F.

Holding each shrimp by the tail, dip the shrimp in the beaten egg wash to coat all over. Dredge the egg-coated shrimp in the flour mixture, coating all but the tail segment. Dip the shrimp in the egg once again, coating all of the flour-covered surfaces with egg. Use a spoon to make certain that the egg sticks to the floured shrimp.

Place the coated shrimp in the coconut and panko breadcrumb mixture. Using another spoon or a fork, totally cover the shrimp with the crunchy mixture by turning the shrimp over, burying it again, and pressing it down into the breadcrumb mixture to make sure that both sides are loaded with as much crunchy coating as possible.

Carefully place each shrimp into the deep fryer basket, lining the bottom (do not place in the oil yet). Unlike many other recipes that involve deep frying, in this case each shrimp can lightly touch each other, but don't overcrowd them.

When you have a batch of shrimp in your fryer basket and the oil is at 375°F, it's now time for the magic! Descend the basket into the hot oil. The frying process should take no more than 2 to 3 minutes.

Serve with the orange dipping sauce as a dip or topping.

Meat

It used to be that when one thought of meat as a main course, it was usually the routine "meat and potatoes." Well, this chapter blows away that theory! Bill Wyman of The Rolling Stones shares his secrets to making Lamb Chops with Endive Salad (page 74), Donnie Dacus of Chicago takes us to the grill with his Fennel & Anise Grilled Pork Chops (page 88), while Scherrie Payne's Spicy Meatloaf (page 86) is nothing short of awesome. For a European masterpiece, flashy pianist and rocker Havasi presents a classic Hungarian Goulash (page 80) from his home country, right down to the handmade noodles.

Credit: Felipe Echerri

Credit: Dave Marken

LEFT: I was still in college when I first interviewed Scherrie Payne for a magazine article. Here, Scherrie and I are at the West Hollywood nightclub Rage, where we gathered for her CD release party in 2016.
RIGHT: While I was compiling recipes for this book, I met Hungarian classical and rock pianist, Balázs Havasi. Here we are at his smashingly successful American concert debut at Carnegie Hall, New York City, in 2015.

Lamb Chops with Endive Salad

Bill Wyman of The Rolling Stones

When I joined Mary Wilson in Europe for her 2014 rock & roll road tour with Bill Wyman's Rhythm Kings, Bill gave me this great recipe!

Yield:

Serves 4 people

Ingredients

Lamb and marinade:
1 tablespoon minced fresh garlic
1 tablespoon chopped fresh rosemary leaves
1 teaspoon dried herbes de Provence (basil, thyme, lavender, fennel)
1 teaspoon salt
½ teaspoon ground black pepper
¼ teaspoon cayenne (red) pepper
½ cup fresh squeezed lemon juice
¼ cup olive oil
8 lamb loin chops (or 8 lamb rib chops or shank chops, or 4 lamb shoulder chops)

Salad:
4 to 6 heads of endive
1 cup crumbled bleu cheese
½ cup walnuts

Balsamic vinaigrette dressing:
¼ cup balsamic vinegar
¾ cup olive oil
¼ cup fresh squeezed lemon juice
1 tablespoon honey
1 teaspoon salt
1 teaspoon ground black pepper

In a bowl, combine the garlic, chopped rosemary leaves, herbes de Provence, salt, ground black pepper, cayenne pepper, lemon juice, and olive oil. Mix together, and pour into a zippered food storage bag. Add the raw lamb chops, coat the meat evenly with the marinade, and let stand in the refrigerator for 1 hour.

While the meat is marinating, prepare the salad. Cut the leaves of the endive to form spears of lettuce. Add the bleu cheese and walnuts, and refrigerate until it is time to serve. In a bowl or jar, add all the dressing ingredients and mix well.

Preheat oven to 350°F. Take the lamb chops out of the bag. Grill them either on a barbecue grill or using a stovetop grill pan (or frying pan). Sear both sides of the lamb for approximately 3 or 4 minutes per side. Transfer the meat to a baking dish, and place in the oven for 3 to 8 minutes. Add several spoonfuls of marinating liquid—complete with garlic and rosemary chunks—on top of the meat while in the oven to assure more moisture and flavor. If you want the lamb pink in the middle, cook for 3 minutes; if you like lamb cooked throughout, give it a full 8 minutes.

Assemble salad, and serve with these delicious lamb chops à la Bill Wyman!

Roasted Lamb Shoulder
Pete Filleul of Climax Blues Band

I have been friends with Pete Filleul since the 1970s when we were in New York City. At the time, he was the keyboard player of The Climax Blues Band. I hadn't seen him in ages until we were both in Los Angeles in 2014. For this book, he shares this very British favorite of his. He is also very specific about how it is made and what it should be served with. I say, "Excellent call, Pete!"

INGREDIENTS

Lamb:

1 tablespoon salt

1 tablespoon ground black pepper

3 tablespoons of dried oregano

5 lb bone-in lamb shoulder

1 tube (4 oz) garlic paste

Potatoes:

½ cup olive oil

4 large cubed potatoes, skins attached

1 teaspoon salt

1 teaspoon ground black pepper

¼ cup chopped chives

Salad:

1 head iceberg, romaine, or Boston lettuce

1 slivered yellow or purple onion

6 to 8 sliced black or green olives

1 sliced lemon

¼ cup olive oil

¼ cup balsamic vinegar

Yield:

SERVES 4 TO 6 PEOPLE AS A COMPLETE MEAL

Preheat oven to 300°F. In a small bowl, combine the salt, black pepper, and dried oregano. Place the lamb roast in a large roasting pan, fat side down. Rub the meaty side with the salt rub, then smear with garlic puree.

If you are using a pan with a lid, cover with the lid. If it is an open pot or baking dish, cover with aluminum foil. Place in the oven for 5 hours. Remove the lid or aluminum foil, and place the roast back in the oven for 1 hour.

According to Pete's specifications: "Serve with potatoes browned in olive oil or goose fat." Taking his lead, in the last ½ hour of the lamb cooking process, add olive oil to a large frying pan and potatoes. Pan fry over medium-high heat with salt and pepper. Pete likes them garnished with chopped chives.

With regard to the finishing touch to his perfect lamb dinner, Pete instructs, "Serve it with a chopped green salad, with lettuce, slivers of onion, black or green olives, and slices of lemon, with a simple oil and balsamic vinegar dressing." To create the dressing, simply whisk together the olive oil and vinegar.

Beef Shabu Shabu
Duncan Faure of The Bay City Rollers

Shabu shabu is Japanese hot pot, a way of cooking meat and vegetables in a broth, with rice on the side. According to Duncan Faure, whom I have known since the 1970s, "Shabu shabu from The Bay City Rollers days at Imperial Gardens—that's my favorite recipe. And of course, some ass-kicking rock & roll after that."

Ingredients

4 cups water, to boil the rice

2 cups white or brown rice

Water, to boil the noodles

6 oz bean thread noodles (or other rice noodles)

8 cups water, to prepare soup

4 sheets (6 inches each) dried kombu (dried seaweed)

¼ cup Japanese sake

2 cups napa cabbage, cut into bite-size pieces

4 large stemmed, quartered shiitake mushrooms

2 scallions, cut diagonally into ½-inch-thick slices

1 container (12 oz) extra-firm tofu, cut into 1-inch cubes

2 cups fresh spinach

12 to 16 oz beef steak, cut into ⅛-inch-thick slices

To serve:

Ponzu sauce*

Yield:
Serves 4 to 6 people

To prepare the rice, boil 4 cups of water, add the rice, cover, turn down to a simmer, and cook for 20 minutes. Boil water and prepare the bean thread or rice noodles according to the package instructions. Drain and set aside.

Boil 8 cups water for the soup, add kombu, and continue to boil for 10 minutes. Remove the kombu and add the sake. Add the cabbage, mushrooms, scallions, tofu, and spinach. Continue to boil together for 2 to 5 minutes. Add noodles and the sliced beef to the boiling broth at the very end.

Remove the pot from the heat and serve the soup and its contents in large soup bowls. Accompany the soup bowl with a small bowl of white or brown rice. Serve with ponzu sauce.

NOTE: If you want to fully replicate the cook-it-yourself-at-the-table atmosphere of shabu shabu restaurants at home, invest in a portable electric single-burner cooking element. Everyone at the table can be equipped with chopsticks to do their own piece-by-piece cooking in the traditional Japanese style. Start by cooking the raw ingredients in the broth first, followed by the rest.

* Ponzu sauce is a citrusy variety of soy sauce and is available at Asian markets and most grocery stores that have an Asian section. It typically comes in both lemon and lime flavors.

Hungarian Goulash
Havasi

If you are going to make Hungarian goulash, who better to go to for a recipe than classical pianist and rocking musical genius Havasi? I first met him at his Carnegie Hall debut in New York City in 2015. He not only makes incredible music but also knows amazing food as well. According to Havasi, "This is the real, genuine Hungarian goulash."

YIELD:
SERVES 6 OR MORE PEOPLE AS
A MAIN COURSE

INGREDIENTS

3 tablespoons lard or olive oil

5 diced medium onions

1 oz water

5 tablespoons sweet Hungarian paprika

3 teaspoons salt

2 teaspoons ground black pepper

2 tablespoons caraway seeds

3¼ lb beef, cut in bite-sized cubes

2 cloves chopped garlic

1 oz water

2½ quarts (10 cups) water

4 diced tomatoes

5 medium sliced carrots

2 medium sliced parsnips

2 large cubed potatoes

CSIPETKE (PINCHED NOODLES):

1 beaten egg

2 tablespoons water

¼ teaspoon salt

6 tablespoons flour

To serve:

1 cup sour cream

½ cup chopped chives (optional)

1 sliced hot pepper (optional)

1 loaf hard crusted bread

In a large pot, add the lard and sauté the onions until softened. Add 1 oz water to the pot, then add the paprika, salt, pepper, and caraway seeds, and stir. Add the beef and garlic, and cook at medium-high heat until beef is browned, about 10 minutes.

Add an additional 1 oz water, turn down the heat, and continue cooking the beef. After another 10 minutes, add 2½ quarts of water, bring to a boil, turn down the heat, and continue to cook for 1 hour.

Add the tomatoes, carrots, parsnips, and potatoes, and continue to cook for 30 minutes or until the vegetables are tender.

Make csipetke from scratch while the goulash cooks. Combine beaten egg, water,

salt, and flour. Stir into a dough, and knead for 2 minutes. Wrap in plastic wrap, and let rest for 30 minutes. In the last 15 minutes of the goulash cooking time, roll out the dough and make little pinched balls of pasta or sliced slivers. Boil the csipetke in the broth.

When the goulash is done, serve in individual bowls with a large spoonful of sour cream on top and chopped chives (optional). Also, if desired you can garnish it with a slice of hot red pepper (optional). Serve with a loaf of hard crusted bread.

Pot Roast
WALTER EGAN

"This is one of my absolute favorite dishes," says Walter Egan.
"I always loved my grandma's pot roast!"

YIELD:

SERVES 6 TO 8 PEOPLE

INGREDIENTS

⅓ cup olive oil

3 lb beef pot roast*

2 to 3 large peeled and slivered onions

10 to 12 cloves peeled garlic

6 to 8 cleaned and quartered white, gold, or copper potatoes

6 to 8 cleaned halved and lengthwise-sliced carrots

4 tablespoons salt

4 tablespoons ground black pepper

6 to 8 sprigs fresh rosemary

GARNISH:

6 to 8 sprigs additional fresh rosemary (optional)

DIRECTIONS

Preheat the oven to 350°F. In a large pot, add olive oil and heat over medium-high heat. Add the flattest side of the beef, and brown the meat until there is a nice crust. Proceed to brown all of the sides.

When the exposed sides of the beef are browned and crispy, remove from the pot and set aside. The oil at this point should be brown with bits of beef and beef fat. Add the onions and garlic, sauté them, and then remove from the pot and set aside. Using the same oil and beef fat, add the raw potatoes and carrots and mix to coat.

Coat all sides of the outside of the browned beef with salt and pepper. If you are using a large oven-safe lidded pot, return the beef to the pot, surround it with the vegetables, sprinkle with whole rosemary sprigs or leaves, and cover with the lid. If you are using a large oven-proof glass or metal pan, cover with aluminum foil.

Place the covered pot or pan in the middle of the oven. Cook for 3 hours. Remove and let sit, while still covered, for 5 to 10 minutes. Slice and serve the beef with the vegetables, and garnish with additional fresh sprigs of rosemary (optional).

NOTE: Although the recipe is for pot roast, the meat can be any one of several cuts of beef. At the butcher or grocery store, you may find it labeled as a "pot roast" cut; you can also use beef shoulder, chuck roast, or boneless roast. Actually, any thick cut of beef you choose will work.

Leg of Lamb à la Chonita
MARILYN McGOO OF THE FIFTH DIMENSION

"This is a great recipe from our housekeeper, Chonita," Marilyn says. I had never made leg of lamb before Marilyn gave me this amazing recipe. I tried it out at a dinner party, and what was left over was barely enough to make a sandwich with! If making lamb sounds like a daunting task, these simple directions could not make it any easier or more impressive.

YIELD:

SERVES 8 TO 12 PEOPLE

INGREDIENTS
1½ cups Worcestershire sauce

½ cup Dijon mustard

¾ cup chopped fresh ginger

¾ cup minced or finely cut fresh garlic

2 teaspoons salt

2 teaspoons ground black pepper

5 lb leg of lamb

Combine Worcestershire sauce, mustard, ginger, garlic, salt, and pepper. Place leg of lamb and marinade in a large zippered plastic bag and marinate. Place in the refrigerator overnight for the spice mix to permeate the meat.

The next day, preheat oven to 350°F. Remove the lamb from the plastic bag, and place in a baking dish with the marinating liquid. Bake one side of the meat for 30 minutes, uncovered. Remove from the oven, turn over, and return to the oven for 30 additional minutes, uncovered.

Cover the pan and the lamb with aluminum foil or a baking dish lid. Reduce the heat from 350 to 300°F. Return the lamb to the oven and continue baking. The key to this recipe is to bake the lamb for an additional 30 minutes per pound. Five pounds of lamb will take a total of 3½ hours to cook (30 minutes uncovered, turn over, 30 minutes uncovered, then 2½ hours covered).

When the lamb comes out of the oven, there is no need to slice it because it will be, as Marilyn explains, "fall-off-the-bone tender, and extremely well-spiced."

NOTE: I chose to make an accompanying gravy for this lamb recipe. This great wine-flavored sauce works perfectly on this delicious, spicy lamb.

Ingredients
8 tablespoons butter
6 tablespoons flour
3 cups chicken broth (made with chicken stock concentrate)
1 cup port wine

Directions
In a medium size cooking pot, melt the butter and flour over medium heat, while stirring constantly, making a roux. When it turns a golden brown, slowly add the chicken broth and port wine. Keep stirring with a whisk until it is nice and thick. If you want more saltiness and body, add more chicken broth to the gravy.

Spicy Meatloaf
SCHERRIE PAYNE OF THE SUPREMES

It was at a gala party for Scherrie's CD release at Rage discotheque in West Hollywood that the ever-charming Ms. Payne dictated to me her recipe for an incredibly flavorful meatloaf. I have known Scherrie since she first joined The Supremes in the 1970s. She has always brought boundless energy to everything she does, and this rocking meatloaf lives up to its spicy promise. Accompany with a vegetable and salad.

YIELD:
SERVES 10 TO 12 PEOPLE

INGREDIENTS

5 Italian sausages

1 lb ground beef

1 lb ground turkey

2 cups breadcrumbs

3 eggs

1 package (1 oz) dry onion soup mix

3 tablespoons creamy horseradish

3 tablespoons Worcestershire sauce

¼ cup ketchup (or tomato sauce)

2 tablespoons minced garlic*

1 cup or 1 large diced onion

1 cup or 1 large diced green pepper

1 teaspoon paprika

1 teaspoon dry mustard

1 teaspoon chili powder

1 teaspoon Jamaican allspice

1 teaspoon seasoned salt

1 teaspoon ground black pepper

1 can (10.5 oz) cream of mushroom soup

1 package (approximately 1 oz) dry brown gravy mix

TO SERVE:

Ketchup or barbecue sauce (optional)

* Scherrie says, "I like to use the minced garlic that comes in a jar."

Preheat oven to 450°F. Take the casing off of the Italian sausages. Add the sausage meat to a large mixing bowl along with beef, turkey, breadcrumbs, eggs, onion soup mix, creamy horseradish, Worcestershire sauce, ketchup, minced garlic, onion, green pepper, paprika, dry mustard, chili powder, Jamaican allspice, seasoned salt, and black pepper. You can start stirring the ingredients with a large spoon or a spatula, but the best method is to mix it together by hand, like kneading dough.

Scherrie instructs, "Form it into a loaf. Bake at 450°F for 15 minutes, then reduce the heat to 350°F and bake for 45 minutes. Remove it from the oven. Mix together cream of mushroom soup and dry brown gravy mix. Pour the mixture over the top of the meatloaf, and then return to the oven at 450°F for 15 more minutes."

Serve with ketchup or barbecue sauce (optional).

Fennel & Anise Grilled Pork Chops

Donnie Dacus of Chicago

Donnie was an integral part of the group Chicago for several years in the 1980s. He played the role of "Woof" in the film *Hair* and has toured with several top rock stars. (I was actually an extra in this film–in the one scene that was cut, the song "Frank Mills.") Donnie told me that he was on a tour with Stephen Stills in France when he came across this unforgettable pork chop recipe that he was determined to replicate.

Yield:

Serves 2 people

Ingredients

4 cups water

½ cup salt

½ cup sugar

2 bone-in rib pork chops (6 to 8 oz each)*

2 teaspoons ground fennel seed

1 teaspoon garlic powder

1 teaspoon onion powder

1 tablespoon anise oil

Equipment to make pork chops

Donnie-Dacus-outdoor-grill style:

1 outdoor charcoal grill (for indoor cooking: stove top grill pan)

Water-soaked hickory wood chips (or other fruit wood chips)

1 cast iron frying pan

1 digital meat thermometer

In a bowl or shallow baking dish, mix the water, salt, and sugar, and brine the pork chops in it for 1 hour. Start an outdoor charcoal grill with the water-soaked hickory wood chips while the pork chops soak (you can also grill this indoors on a stove top grill pan). Preheat oven to 400°F. After about 50 minutes of brining time, insert a cast iron frying pan into the preheated oven to heat it up.

When the brining is done, the outdoor grill is ready, the hickory chips are smoking, and the cast iron pan is heated, remove the pork chops from the brine. Mix together ground fennel seed, garlic powder, and onion powder, and sprinkle onto the pork chops.

According to Donnie: "When you are ready for action and you have seasoned those chops, go for it." Grill pork chops on the grill, 5 minutes on each side, leaving blackened grill marks on both sides of the meat. Donnie says, "Put 'em on for a few minutes at an angle of 30 degrees to the left and then 30 degrees to the right. We're looking for perfection here! Don't overcook or burn your chops. You'll get the hang of it."

Remove the pork chops from the grill. Place the preheated cast iron pan on the grill, put the pork chops in it, and continue cooking. Using the digital meat thermometer, cook until the internal temperature of the chops reaches 155 to 160°F. When the pork chops reach the desired temperature, remove the frying pan. If you are making this indoors in the oven, it will take around 25 to 30 minutes. You can cut into the pork to determine its degree of doneness.

Using a cooking brush, lightly brush both sides of the chops with anise oil, and serve.

* Donnie recommends: "Purchase two separate bone-in rib chops. Don't let them sell you anything but. Most stores don't even know what it is. It is commonly used for pork crown standing rib roast. Yum on that!"

Stuffed Hatch Chile Peppers
MARK BEGO

I spend a lot of time in Tucson, Arizona, and I wanted to come up with a creative recipe for uniquely spicy Hatch chile peppers, and this bacon-wrapped fantasy rocks it! These great peppers are also known as Anaheim peppers.

YIELD:
8 TO 12 STUFFED PEPPERS,
SERVES 4 TO 6 PEOPLE

INGREDIENTS

3 tablespoons olive oil
2 chopped onions
1 lb ground beef
½ cup tomato sauce
½ cup water
1 teaspoon paprika
1 teaspoon salt
½ teaspoon ground black pepper
1 teaspoon chili powder
1 teaspoon ground cumin
½ teaspoon onion powder
½ teaspoon red cayenne pepper
8 to 12 Hatch chile peppers
2 cups shredded Cheddar cheese
16 to 24 strips bacon

TOPPINGS:
1 bottle of your favorite hot sauce
8 oz sour cream (optional)

DIRECTIONS

In a medium-sized frying pan, heat the olive oil. Sauté the onions. When they are beginning to soften, remove from the pan, and set aside.

Over medium-high heat, brown the ground beef in the same pan. When the beef is browned, drain it. Add to the pan tomato sauce, water, paprika, salt, pepper, chili powder, ground cumin, onion powder, and cayenne pepper. Return the cooked onions to the pan. Stir together and simmer for 15 to 20 minutes, until it thickens up.

With a small sharp knife, slit one side of the Hatch chile pepper from stem to tip. Cut a 1-inch slit ¼ inch away from the stem, leaving the top of the pepper intact. Open the pepper up and remove the seeds and strings from the interior.

Stuff the peppers almost full with the meat mixture, and fill the rest of the cavity with shredded Cheddar cheese. Close the peppers up and wrap them from top to bottom with two slices of bacon for each one.

Bake in a tempered glass or metal baking dish at 350°F for 1 hour. Serve with hot sauce and a big glob of sour cream (optional) to balance out the heat of the pepper, cayenne, and hot sauce.

Pork Dan Dan Noodles
Mark Bego

This spicy noodle dish is a huge hit in China. You can also make this vegan by using meatless soy crumbles.

Yield:
Serves 2 to 4 people

Ingredients
2 tablespoons vegetable or olive oil
3 tablespoons minced garlic
4 tablespoons minced fresh ginger
1 lb ground pork
2 tablespoons rice wine vinegar
3 teaspoons Chinese five spice
1 teaspoon sugar
1 teaspoon salt
1 cup vegetable broth
2 tablespoons Chinese black vinegar
2 tablespoons chili oil
2 tablespoons sesame oil
4 tablespoons Chinese sesame paste
2 tablespoons oyster sauce
2 soy sauce
1 teaspoon crushed red pepper flakes
1 teaspoon ground Chinese black pepper
10 oz Chinese noodles

Garnish:
2 additional tablespoons chili oil
8 to 10 sprigs of Chinese spinach or yu choy leaves
2 to 4 diced scallions

Directions

Heat olive oil in a frying pan, add the minced garlic and ginger, and sauté. When the garlic and ginger begin to cook, add the ground pork. When it is browned and has a crumbled texture, add rice wine vinegar, Chinese five spice, sugar, and salt. Let it simmer together, about 3 minutes, and set it aside.

In a saucepan, add the vegetable broth, black vinegar, chili oil, sesame oil, sesame paste, oyster sauce, soy sauce, red pepper flakes, and black pepper. Cook on medium heat, constantly stirring for about 5 minutes. The sauce will go from being clumpy to a smooth and consistent liquid. After it has come together, keep the sauce warm at very low heat. In the meantime, start a pot of water boiling, add the noodles, cook for 5 minutes. Drain and set aside.

When everything is ready, assemble in separate serving bowls or in one large serving bowl: pour several spoonfuls of sauce in the bottom of the bowl, followed by some ground pork, and add the noodles on the top. Top with more pork and sauce. Draw a circle of chili oil around the bowl of noodles to give an oily orange glow. Top with raw Chinese spinach or yu choy leaves and diced scallions.

Mongolian Beef
MARK BEGO

For a great three-course Chinese dinner, make this dish with Chinese Cold Sesame Noodles (page 142) and Lobster Egg Rolls (page 116).

YIELD:

SERVES 4 PEOPLE

INGREDIENTS

SAUCE:

5 tablespoons hoisin sauce

2 tablespoons oyster sauce

3 tablespoons soy sauce

2 tablespoons vinegar (apple cider, rice wine, or white vinegar)

1 tablespoon cornstarch

RICE:

2 cups water

1 cup white rice

BEEF:

½ cup olive oil

8 stalks scallions

6 cloves chopped garlic

2 tablespoons chopped ginger

½ cup cornstarch

1 lb thinly sliced beef (flank steak, sliced sirloin, or any beef will work)

½ cup whole dried red chili peppers*

In a small bowl place the hoisin sauce, oyster sauce, soy sauce, vinegar, and cornstarch. Stir together, and set aside.

To make the rice, pour water into a covered pot, and bring to a boil. When the water boils, add the white rice, replace the lid, and reduce the heat to the lowest setting. Allow to simmer for 20 minutes.

In a wok or frying pan, place ¼ cup of olive oil in the pan, reserving the rest for later. Add the scallions, garlic, and ginger. Sauté until tender, and remove from oil. Put the cornstarch on a dinner plate or cutting board. Using your hands or a set of tongs, dredge the sliced strips of beef through the cornstarch until covered with a sticky white dusting.

Place the beef strips individually into the heated olive oil and brown them, being careful to keep the majority of the cornstarch intact. Ideally, you want a brown crunchiness to the outside of the beef. Add extra olive oil as needed. Cook in batches until the beef is browned.

Add the beef, scallions, garlic, and ginger back to the still-hot wok or frying pan. Then add the sauce and the dried red chili peppers. Gently stir, mixing everything together until the sauce thickens, about 3 minutes. Serve atop cooked white rice.

*The dried red chili peppers will impart a definite spiciness to the dish. However, do not eat them unless you know what you are doing; they are super spicy!

Fish & Seafood

Whether you live next to an ocean, a lake, or a river, or live in the middle of the desert, fresh seafood and fish are readily available nearly everywhere. In this chapter, you will find precision high-cuisine recipes like Susaye Greene's Bouillabaisse (page 100), as well as ones that are very easy to prepare. Shawn Stockman of Boyz II Men demonstrates an excellent way to cook Ginger Red Sea Bass (page 102). If salmon is your passion, Paul Antonelli of Animotion, August Darnell of Kid Creole & The Coconuts, and Sean Lennon have shared three variations that are all amazing—and totally different.

Credit: Richard Nichols

Credit: Felipe Echerri

LEFT: Mary Wilson and I with the phenomenal Freda Payne celebrating Freda's headlining concert performance at The Willis Theater in Beverly Hills, California, January 7, 2017. Coincidentally, all three of us are from Detroit, Michigan!

RIGHT: If ever there was a rock star whose middle name has to be "Fun," it is Paul Antonelli of Animotion. Here we are at the West Hollywood restaurant, Pump, in 2017.

Ginger Scallion Salmon
Sean Lennon

In Tucson, Arizona, there is a great downtown rock club located in the historic Congress Hotel, with a warm and intimate performance room called The Club Congress. When I went there recently to see Sean Lennon and his band The Ghost of the Saber Tooth Tiger, I was immediately impressed with his engrossing performing style, as well as his charmingly warm and low-key charisma. Something instinctively told me that he was not only a rocker but also a foodie, too. Well, I was right! Sean had a great salmon recipe in mind and very definite ideas on how to make it. "When I say 'The ginger should be sliced thin,' I mean, 'very thin,'" he told me. However, he does not recommend using a mandolin for uniform slices. "You do it by hand," he says. "I don't like everything so uniform." Serve with your favorite vegetable or salad.

YIELD:

SERVES 4 PEOPLE

INGREDIENTS
1 cup fresh ginger
1 cup scallions
⅛ cup olive oil
4 salmon filets, with or without skin
¼ cup soy sauce

DIRECTIONS

Peel or cut the skin off of the ginger. With a very sharp knife, carefully cut the ginger into thin coin-sized slices. Then, cut the slices into what Sean describes as "spaghetti strips." Next, Sean says, "Chop the scallions vertically into thin slices."

In a large frying pan or grilling pan, heat olive oil over medium-high heat. If your salmon filets are skinless, place them meat side down to sear them. If your salmon has skin, start cooking with the meat side down and the skin side up.

After 3 minutes on that side, turn the salmon filets over. Sean instructs: "Smother the salmon with a blanket of ginger and scallions. Cover the pan with the lid for 5 minutes. Then sprinkle soy sauce into the pan, and heat for 10 seconds, covered. Whatever you do, do not burn the soy sauce. You know how bad it smells burned; you want to avoid that." I gave the fish closer to a full minute with the soy sauce to make sure the flavor steamed into the salmon. I served it with additional soy sauce to give it an added Asian-flavored tang.

Bouillabaisse
SUSAYE GREENE OF THE SUPREMES

Bouillabaisse is truly the king of all fish soups. Here, Susaye Greene "rocks" this classic seafood dish. Although the amount of ingredients makes it look dauntingly complicated, it is quite easy to make. For a richer seafood flavor, boil the broth with additional fish bones and lobster or shrimp shells removed from the flesh. When it comes time to add the seafood, you can also add scallops, crawfish, crabmeat, or crab legs.

YIELD:
SERVES 4 TO 6 PEOPLE

INGREDIENTS

1 tablespoon extra virgin olive oil

1 large chopped onion

2 to 3 medium chopped carrots

2 large stalks celery

1 cup chicken or fish stock

1 sprig fresh rosemary

1 bay leaf

2 to 3 cloves chopped garlic

2 mashed anchovies

4 cups white wine

¼ cup water

3 to 4 sprigs saffron

4 cups water

3 chopped potatoes

¼ cup sliced or chopped fresh fennel root

3 large chopped tomatoes

1 lb dense fish (such as cod, salmon, red snapper, plaice, ling)

½ lb mussels

½ lb clams

1 lobster, cut up in the shell

1 lb shrimp

¼ cup chopped fresh basil

1 fresh lime

GARLIC BREADCRUMBS:

1 cup breadcrumbs

4 tablespoons water

4 minced garlic cloves

1 teaspoon sea salt, to taste

½ teaspoon red pepper flakes

4 tablespoons olive oil

Add olive oil to a large pot, along with the onion. Sauté for a few minutes, then add carrots and celery. Continue cooking for 5 minutes. Add the chicken or fish stock, whole rosemary sprig, and bay leaf. Allow to simmer a few minutes, then add garlic, mashed anchovies, and white wine. Bring to a boil, turn down heat, and continue to cook.

In a small pot, add ¼ cup water and saffron. Over medium heat, boil until the water is a strong orange color. Remove the saffron strands, then pour the orange saffron liquid into the stock. Add 4 cups of water, ½ cup at a time. Continue boiling. Add the potatoes, fennel, and tomatoes, and bring to a boil. When the potatoes start to soften, remove the rosemary sprig and bay leaf, and add the fish. Cook for 3 minutes, then add mussels, clams, lobster, and shrimp. Continue boiling for 4 or 5 minutes.

Susaye says, "At the end, I add fresh basil, and a squeeze of lime. The entire cooking time is a bit over 1 hour from start to finish."

As the fish and seafood cooks, prepare a garlic paste of breadcrumbs by mixing together breadcrumbs, 4 tablespoons water, four minced garlic cloves, salt, red pepper flakes, and 4 tablespoons of olive oil. Add a tablespoon of this mix to each serving bowl of bouillabaisse. This is for both thickness and flavor.

Susaye adds, "I serve this Bouillabaisse with a good fresh crusty bread of choice, a French or Italian loaf. Garlic bread is also good. This dish can also be served with rice or pasta, if you wish."

Ginger Red Sea Bass
Shawn Stockman of Boyz ll Men

At the Kentucky Derby, Shawn Stockman and I were both in line to place our bets, and the conversation turned to food. When I asked him for a recipe for this cookbook, he instantly started talking about this red sea bass he had recently had, with a side of garlic noodles. The way he spoke about it, I knew this was going to be a winner. This recipe is not only excellent, but also very easy to make. Serve with Shawn's amazing Asian Fusion Garlic Noodles (page 128).

Yield:

Serves 6 people

Ingredients
6 filets red sea bass, with or without skin
1 teaspoon salt
1 teaspoon pepper
¼ cup olive oil
2 tablespoons soy sauce
¼ cup fresh ginger, sliced into matchsticks
3 thinly sliced garlic cloves
1 cup deseeded thinly sliced red bell pepper
1 cup lengthwise-sliced scallions

Topping:
Additional soy sauce

Directions

Preheat oven to 250°F. If the sea bass has the skin attached, with a sharp knife, cut three slits into the skin side of each filet. Sprinkle both sides of the fish with salt and pepper.

Add olive oil to a large frying pan over medium-high heat. Add the sea bass. If the skin is attached, place skin-side-down first. Cook for approximately 5 minutes, until the skin or the first side of the exposed fish is crispy. Flip over each filet and fry the fish on the other side for 2 or 3 minutes. Add soy sauce to the pan, lid it, and steam the fish in soy sauce for 1 additional minute. Remove the fish from the frying pan, and set aside. Place the cooked fish in the preheated oven to keep warm.

Add the ginger, garlic, and red bell peppers to the frying pan, and stir-fry them 2 minutes. Add the scallion slivers, stir an additional 1 minute, and remove the pan from the heat.

Arrange the sea bass filets on a serving dish or on individual plates. Sprinkle the fish with the colorful array of slivered vegetables, and serve immediately with soy sauce.

Gumbo
Freda Payne

If you like spicy seafood, this gumbo is right up your alley. Although it takes some concentration to create, the results are stunning. With seafood, chicken, and sausage, this is the ticket to a truly delicious New Orleans treat. Hats off to Freda!

YIELD:
8 TO 10 SERVINGS

INGREDIENTS

3 to 4 tablespoons flour

8 tablespoons (1 stick) butter

2 cups water

1½ cups chopped onion

1½ cups chopped celery
    (including the leaves)

1½ cups chopped green pepper

1½ cups fresh or frozen sliced
    okra

2 to 3 bay leaves

1 can (28 oz) crushed tomatoes

½ cup chopped fresh parsley

3 tablespoons gumbo filé
    powder

1 teaspoon ground sage

1 tablespoon salt

2 teaspoons ground black
    pepper

1 teaspoon cayenne pepper

1 whole skinned chicken (or 4
    cut up breasts, or 6 thighs
    and legs)

1 large sliced beef and pork sausage

1 quart water

4 to 6 cups water (to prepare the rice)

2 to 3 cups white rice

1 lb shrimp

1 cut up Dungeness crab (or 1 lb king crab legs or 1
    lb blue crabs)

In a large pot, add the flour and butter, and stir continuously over medium heat until it thickens into a roux. Freda says, "I like to make it a dark brown for taste." When it is thickened and brown, slowly stir in 2 cups water until it is a smooth, thick, gravy-like mixture.

Add chopped onion, celery, green pepper, okra, bay leaves, crushed tomatoes, parsley, gumbo filé powder, ground sage, salt, black pepper, and cayenne pepper. Stir together over medium heat. Add the chicken, sausage, and 1 quart of water. Bring to a boil. Reduce the heat to low, and simmer for 45 to 50 minutes. Freda suggests you sample the gumbo midway to see if you need more salt or cayenne.

In the last 25 to 30 minutes, prepare the rice so it will be done when the gumbo finishes cooking. Bring 4 cups water to a boil, add 2 cups rice, cover the pot, lower to a slow simmer, and cook 20 minutes. (You can also use 6 cups water for 3 cups rice.)

In the last 10 minutes, add the shrimp and crab, and continue cooking. Serve in large bowls. Freda notes, "Some people like just a little bit of rice in the bottom of the bowl, with the gumbo ladled on top of it, while other people like more rice in it."

Dijon Caper Salmon
PAUL ANTONELLI OF ANIMOTION

Paul Antonelli is one of the most fun and energetic people I have ever met. He never ever does anything halfway, and everything he engages in is done with gusto and excitement. This includes his recipes and cooking. This easy-to-make and delicious recipe for salmon proves his lust for life and his flair for food!

YIELD:

SERVES 4 PEOPLE

INGREDIENTS
2 lb salmon filet, with or without skin
2 to 3 tablespoons olive oil, to grease
1 to 2 tablespoons olive oil, to drizzle
½ teaspoon salt
½ teaspoon ground black pepper (fresh, if possible)
½ to 1 cup Dijon mustard
½ thinly sliced red onion
2 tablespoons capers
1 sprig of chopped fresh dill
2 tomatoes, chopped
Salt, to taste
Ground black pepper, to taste

DIRECTIONS

Preheat oven to 400°F (or 375°F if you are using a convection oven). Place the salmon, skin side down, on a baking sheet that has been lightly covered with 2 or 3 tablespoons olive oil. Drizzle 1 or 2 tablespoons olive oil on the salmon, and evenly spread it on the surface of the fish. Salt and pepper the salmon.

Slice the salmon into four portions. Spread the Dijon mustard all over the fish. According to Paul, "The Dijon mustard should cover the fish sufficiently." Arrange the red onions on top of the Dijon, and sprinkle the capers and dill over the top. Spread the chopped tomatoes in the baking dish around the base of the fish. Salt and pepper the tomatoes.

Place the baking dish in the center of the oven, and cook for 10 to 12 minutes. Paul suggests, "Check the salmon in the thickest section after 10 minutes. The salmon should be the slightest pink. If not, put it back in the oven for another 1 or 2 minutes, and check it again." If you like the edges on your salmon slightly browned and the fish firmly cooked, go up to 15 minutes bake time.

Pull the salmon out of the oven, let it sit for 1 to 2 minutes, and serve.

Tuna Bake
MARI WILSON

According to Mari Wilson, "This is a great winter warmer–comfort food. All of us in my family love it. Very filling, very satisfying, and very easy. Also, inexpensive! A glass of red wine goes down like a treat with this." Right on, Mari!

YIELD:

SERVES 3 TO 4 PEOPLE

INGREDIENTS

Water, to fill a saucepan

¼ teaspoon salt

2 peeled and cubed potatoes

1 cup diced carrots

1 tablespoon vegetable oil (optional)

1 chopped onion

2 cloves chopped garlic

1 can (14.5 oz) chopped tomatoes

1 teaspoon marmite, vegemite, or vegetable bouillon concentrate

¼ cup hot water (to dissolve)

1 can (12 oz) tuna fish

2 tablespoons butter

2 tablespoons cream cheese

2 tablespoons whole milk

2 cups grated sharp Cheddar or Parmesan cheese

To SERVE:

Green vegetables (broccoli or sprouts)

Fill a large saucepan with water. Add salt and potatoes. Boil for approximately 20 minutes, until the potatoes are soft and ready to mash. According to Mari, "If you're adding carrots, put them in a pan of salted boiling water, and simmer for about 10 minutes."

Meanwhile, preheat the oven to 450°F. In a deep frying pan, fry the onion and garlic in oil until soft and transparent. Add the canned tomatoes. Melt the marmite, vegemite, or vegetable bouillon concentrate in boiled water. Add this liquid mixture and tuna to the pan. If there are any large pieces of tuna, break them up. Bring the mixture to a boil, and pour it into a casserole dish.

If you used carrots, drain and arrange them on top. Combine the potatoes with butter, cream cheese, and milk, and mash the mixture. Spoon the mashed potato onto the tuna and tomatoes.

According to Mari, "Grate the cheese on the top, and place in the oven to broil for 5 minutes until browned and crispy." While Mari suggests setting the oven to "broil," I was using a tempered glass pan, so I set my oven to 450°F, giving the casserole 15 minutes to bake and for the cheese to brown. Either method you choose, Mari's recipe is brilliant, and it is a great way to take a large can of tuna into a whole new stratosphere of taste!

Mari says, "Serve with green vegetables, such as broccoli and sprouts."

Cooked Cabbage & Shrimp
Thelma Houston

According to Thelma, "This is a very simple, but totally delicious, way to serve cooked cabbage." She suggests a couple of cooking tips: "You can use either one red bell pepper or one yellow bell pepper in this dish. Or, you can also use one of each for additional color. When you cut the scallions, cut them into 1-inch pieces." This is a surefire way to make cooked cabbage instantly exciting.

Yield:
Serves 6 to 8 people as a side dish, and 3 to 4 people as a low-calorie main course

Ingredients
1 head cabbage
¼ cup olive oil
1 chopped red bell pepper
1 chopped yellow bell pepper
8 to 10 chopped scallions
½ lb medium shrimp

Directions

Cut the head of cabbage in half, and cut out and remove the tough heart. Slice the halves of cabbage into ½-inch pieces so they will fall apart in the pot. In a large pot over medium heat, heat olive oil and sauté peppers and scallions until they soften. Next, add the sliced cabbage, continuing to stir and sauté until it softens.

Add the shrimp on top of the cabbage, and lid the pot, continuing to cook until the shrimp turns pink.

NOTE: If you wanted to go totally vegan with this dish, simply substitute the ½ lb shrimp with 7 oz pan-fried tofu cubes.

Seven People Salmon
August Darnell of Kid Creole & The Coconuts

When I first met August Darnell, he was part of the disco group Dr. Buzzard's Original Savannah Band. In the 1980s, August came up with his alter ego, Kid Creole, and along with The Coconuts, he began his second successful musical career. I even appeared as an actor in their first two videos! August's wife, Eva, assures me that salmon fried rice is one of his favorite dishes. Eva says, "I created this dish while in the kitchen at home in Sweden. August and I both loved it, but it didn't really have a name, just 'the salmon rice dish.'" When they had family visit at Christmastime, it had to be expanded to accommodate the number of guests and was finally dubbed "Seven People Salmon."

YIELD:
SERVES 7 PEOPLE, OF COURSE!

INGREDIENTS

4 skinless salmon filets

1 tablespoon soy sauce

2 tablespoons olive oil

1 finely diced red or yellow pepper

1 finely diced red onion

1 peeled and finely diced carrot

1 finely diced zucchini

2 crushed or diced cloves garlic

4 cups water

Salt, to taste (optional)

2 cups white rice

¼ to ½ cup soy sauce

½ teaspoon garlic powder

½ teaspoon ground black pepper

1 egg

¼ cup sliced scallions

Heat a wok to a medium temperature, without oil, and add the salmon filets. Turn them every 1 minute until cooked on the outside. Flake the salmon and continue frying, ensuring they are fully cooked. Add a tablespoon of soy sauce, fry for an extra 1 minute, remove from pan, and set aside. In the same wok, add the olive oil. Add the diced pepper, onion, carrot, and zucchini, and sauté until lightly browned. Add the garlic halfway through so it doesn't burn.

Bring water to a boil, add salt (optional), then add the rice. Once rice is cooked, return the flaked salmon to the vegetables in the wok, and add the rice. Mix salmon, vegetables, and rice, heating it all the way through. Add soy sauce, garlic powder, and black pepper, continually stirring the mixture so it doesn't burn or stick.

Make a well in the center of the rice mixture and crack the egg into it. Stir the egg around with a wooden spoon until cooked, then mix the scrambled egg through the rice mixture. Spoon the fried rice mixture equally into bowls, garnish with sliced scallions, and serve.

Soft-Shell Crabs on Black Linguini
MARK BEGO

> These incredible crabs allow you to eat them shell and all. Atop black squid ink pasta they are just incredible.

YIELD:

SERVES 4 PEOPLE, ALLOWING FOR
2 CRABS PER PERSON

INGREDIENTS

LEMON MARINARA SAUCE:

2 cups chopped onion

2 cups chopped red bell pepper

1 cup chopped celery

¼ cup chopped fresh garlic

¼ cup olive oil

1 can (15 oz) tomato sauce

1 can (14.5 oz) diced tomatoes

1 can (6 oz) tomato paste

1 cup white wine

½ teaspoon salt

½ teaspoon ground black pepper

¼ cup chopped fresh oregano
   leaves

¼ cup chopped fresh basil leaves

2 tablespoons capers

2 tablespoons fresh lemon zest

½ cup fresh lemon juice

PASTA:

Water, to boil pasta

1 lb black linguini (squid ink,
   imported from Italy)

SOFT-SHELL CRABS:

2 cups flour

1 teaspoon salt

1 teaspoon ground black pepper

1 teaspoon ground paprika

2 whole eggs

½ cup olive oil

8 soft-shell crabs (face and gills removed:
   ask your fish merchant to do this for you)

Lemon Marinara Sauce: Add the onion, pepper, celery, garlic, and ¼ cup olive oil to a large saucepan. Sauté vegetables until they soften. Add tomato sauce, diced tomatoes, tomato paste, white wine, salt, pepper, oregano, basil, capers, fresh lemon zest, and fresh lemon juice. Over medium-high heat, stir and bring the sauce to a boil, then turn down to low heat and simmer.

Pasta: Start a pot of water to boil for the pasta. Add black linguini in the boiling water and cook until al dente.

Soft-shell crabs: In a bowl, combine the flour, salt, pepper, and paprika. In another bowl, crack two whole eggs. Beat the eggs together with a fork or whisk. Rinse the soft-shell crab.

In a large frying pan, pour ½ cup olive oil, and heat to medium-high heat. Dip each soft-shell crab in the egg wash, covering the body, legs, and claws with egg. Dredge each crab in the flour mixture. Place them top side down in the frying pan. Cook each crab top side down for 2 minutes, and then flip over to cook on the other side for 3 minutes.

On individual plates or pasta bowls, add black pasta, a generous amount of lemon marinara sauce, and soft-shell crabs on top.

Lobster Egg Rolls
Mark Bego

Serve these with dipping sauces, such as hot Chinese mustard, soy sauce with hot chili oil, sweet and sour sauce, Japanese ponzu sauce, or hoisin sauce.

Yield:
10 to 12 egg rolls

Ingredients

Soy sauce mixture:
2 teaspoons soy sauce
1 tablespoon water
1 tablespoon sugar
1 teaspoon ground black pepper
1 teaspoon Chinese five spice

Lobster filling:
3 tablespoons olive oil
2 tablespoons chopped garlic
2 tablespoons chopped ginger
2½ cups chopped cabbage
¼ cup chopped cilantro
2 tablespoons chopped scallion
½ cup thinly sliced celery
1 cup cooked and coarsely chopped lobster meat

To fry:
Enough olive oil or other cooking oil

Shell:
1 whole egg
10 to 12 egg roll skins

In a small bowl, add the soy sauce, water, sugar, black pepper, and Chinese five spice. Stir together, and set aside.

In a wok or frying pan, add olive oil, garlic, and ginger, and cook for 2 minutes over medium heat. Next, add cabbage, cilantro, scallion, and celery. Stir in the hot oil for 1 minute, then add lobster and the soy sauce mixture. Stir all ingredients together for 1 or 2 minutes, and remove from heat.

Preheat the oven to 250°F. Begin heating the oil to 350 to 375°F in a deep fryer (ideal), or a wok or frying pan if you don't have one. Begin rolling egg rolls 3 minutes ahead of frying. Crack and beat egg in a small mixing bowl. On a clean surface (a cutting board or plate), set down an egg roll skin, with one of the four points facing you. Dip a pastry or basting brush in the beaten egg, and trace a 1-inch-wide line of beaten egg along all 4 outer edges of the egg roll skin. This will serve as "the glue" that will seal the egg roll and keep the filling inside the second it hits the oil.

Carefully put 2 tablespoons of lobster filling in the center of the egg roll skin in a horizontal line, leaving 1 inch of clean egg roll skin on the left and right sides, and several inches at the top and the bottom. Fold the left and right side corners in over the filling. Next, fold up the bottom corner to the level of the filling, and tightly roll upward over the last point of the egg roll skin, making sure the beaten egg "glues" the egg roll together. If need be, tuck in the sides to make sure no part of the filling is exposed.

I strongly suggest you fry in batches of threes: 1) roll three egg rolls, 2) fry immediately, 3) remove from the oil. Repeat the process until you have made 12 egg rolls. Use kitchen tongs or a slotted spoon to handle the hot egg rolls. If you are using a frying pan or wok, turn over the egg roll after about 1 minute. Keep turning the egg rolls so that all sides are thoroughly brown.

When the egg rolls are golden brown, place in the preheated oven as you start on the next batch of 3.

Serve these great egg rolls with your favorite dipping sauces.

Coquille St. Jacques
MARK BEGO

Although making Coquille St. Jacques seems long and involved, it is actually quite easy and totally worth the effort. Accompany it with noodles or rice, a cooked vegetable, and/ or a small salad.

INGREDIENTS

4 tablespoon butter

1 lb bay scallops

2 tablespoons freshly squeezed lemon juice

1 cup white wine

½ cup chopped parsley

½ teaspoon salt

¼ teaspoon cayenne (red) pepper

¼ cup water

¼ cup olive oil

2 chopped shallots

2 cups sliced mushrooms

1 tablespoon chopped garlic

4 tablespoons flour

3 tablespoons butter

½ cup half-and-half or heavy cream

½ cup grated Gruyère cheese

½ cup bread crumbs

6 tablespoons raw white rice (if you are plating in a scallop shell)

YIELD:

4 MAIN COURSE SERVINGS OR 6 APPETIZER-SIZED PORTIONS SERVED IN SCALLOP SHELLS

Grease 4 baking dishes that can accommodate 2 cups of filling each (or use 6 actual scallop shells), using 1 tablespoon butter for each dish. In a saucepan, add scallops, lemon juice, white wine, parsley, salt, cayenne pepper, and water. Over medium to medium-high heat, bring to a boil, and remove from the stove. Remove the scallops from the liquid and set aside. Return the pan to the stove, and turn down the heat to simmer for 10 minutes until the liquid condenses slightly. Remove the liquid and parsley from the pan, and set aside.

Add the olive oil, shallots, mushrooms, and garlic to the same pan. Over medium heat, sauté until tender. Remove from the heat, remove from the pan, and set aside.

Preheat the oven to "broil," placing the upper rack no higher than the middle.

In the same pan, add flour and 3 tablespoons butter, and return to heat, turning back up to medium. Stirring constantly with a spoon or whisk, thicken into a roux. Slowly add back the condensed liquid that was set aside, stirring constantly, until the roux thickens into a gravy.

Add the half-and-half or heavy cream, the set aside scallops, the set aside shallots and mushrooms, and ¼ cup Gruyère cheese. When the mixture is thick, divide the contents of the pan into the 4 baking dishes, or 6 scallop shells. Sprinkle the tops with breadcrumbs, and then top with the second ¼ cup of Gruyère cheese.

Place the baking dishes or shells onto a cooking sheet or pizza pan, and place in the oven. Broil for 5 to 7 minutes. You want the tops to have a nice browned crust, but be careful not to burn them.

Serve the baking dishes atop a plate. To plate the shells, place 1 tablespoon raw white rice in middle of plate, and rest the shell on it.

Pasta

Without a doubt, pasta is one of the most versatile main course ingredients around. Michael McDonald has an incredible recipe for Pasta with Ham, Peas & Parmesan Cheese (page 122) that he fell in love with while in Italy. For a true Italian classic, Lou Christie's totally vegetarian Summer Linguini (page 124) is just the ticket! Jade Starling of Pretty Poison shares her own meaty Jade Lasagna (page 126), while Cherry Vanilla's "Quick and Stiff" Spinach Lasagna (page 132) is a great meatless option. And if you want to go extra meaty, try my Rigatoni Bolognese (page 138). Pasta can go Chinese as well—check out Shawn Stockman's yummy Asian Fusion Garlic Noodles (page 128).

Credit: Alan LaFever

Credit: Derek Storm

LEFT: Me, Mary Wilson, and Michael McDonald, backstage at The Greek Theater in 2016 for his concert.
RIGHT: In February of 2006, I hosted a Valentine's Day party at The Cutting Room in New York City, and three of my favorite rock stars helped me celebrate in style: Randy Jones of The Village People, Lala Brooks of The Crystals, and the legendary "Lightning Strikes" hit-maker Lou Christie.

Pasta with Ham, Peas & Parmesan Cheese
Michael McDonald of The Doobie Brothers

Michael McDonald was one of the nicest men on the planet back in 1976 when I first met him during an interview with Patrick Simmons, also of The Doobie Brothers, and he is just as warm and friendly to this day. In 2014, I ran into him at the Los Angeles International Airport by pure coincidence and was gifted with a wonderful recipe. "I was in Italy recently," Michael says, "and I absolutely fell in love with this pasta, which is pretty simple and just delicious. It is basically ham and Parmesan cheese, and little else. It sometimes has peas in it, which I like, but I also love it without peas, as well. It can be made with lardons or pancetta. It is sort of a peasant dish, often made with the ham from a pig's head."

Yield:

Serves 3 to 4 people

Ingredients
Water, to boil the pasta
½ lb pasta (farfalle, fusilli, ziti, orecchiette, or whatever shape you like)
2 cups cubed or shredded ham, or pancetta
¼ cup olive oil (optional)
1½ cups peas (frozen or fresh)
2 cups grated Parmesan cheese
¼ cup sour cream
Freshly ground black pepper, to taste

Additions (optional):
Sautéed onions
Sautéed portobello mushrooms
Sliced black olives
Chopped flat-leaf parsley, to garnish

Directions

Boil the water for the pasta, and add whatever pasta you like. In a large frying pan, place the ham or pancetta, and begin to brown. If you are using cooked ham, add olive oil; if you are using pancetta, brown it and remove the "bacon grease" that will remain in the pan.

Add the peas, and lightly sauté them together. If the pasta is not done yet, take the frying pan off the heat until is the pasta is ready.

Drain the cooked pasta, add to the frying pan, and return to the heat. Add Parmesan cheese and sour cream, tossing everything together quickly before the cheese begins to clump together. Optional: you can add other ingredients to this pasta, such as sautéed onions, portobello mushrooms, black olives, or flat-leaf parsley.

Serve immediately with freshly ground black pepper on top of it.

Summer Linguini
Lou Christie

When Lou gave me this recipe, the first thing I thought was *Where is the oregano and tomato paste for this?* But when I followed his instructions just as he described it, I was knocked out by the amazing, fresh flavors this "from scratch" recipe packed. Nothing else is needed. Like Lou's 1966 number one hit, "Lightnin' Strikes," this sauce is a lightning storm of truly authentic Italian taste!

YIELD:

SERVES 3 TO 4 PEOPLE

INGREDIENTS

Water, to boil the pasta

¼ teaspoon salt

¼ cup extra virgin olive oil

3 or 4 cloves sliced or diced garlic

4 or 5 large chopped tomatoes (or 6 to 7 medium tomatoes)

4 or 5 freshly ripped basil leaves ("Rip, don't cut," says Lou)

¼ teaspoon dried red pepper flakes (also known as *pepperoncini* in Italian)

1 lb linguini

GARNISHES (OPTIONAL)

1 cup grated or shaved Parmesan cheese

6 to 7 additional shredded basil leaves

DIRECTIONS

Boil a large pot of water and add salt. In a separate pot or frying pan, add olive oil and garlic. Sauté garlic until it starts to brown.

Add chopped tomatoes, basil leaves, and red pepper flakes. As Lou instructs, "Cover and let simmer over low heat for 15 minutes." While this is happening, place the linguini into the water and cook until al dente.

Says Lou, "Drain the pasta, pour your summer sauce over the linguini, and serve. Now, open another bottle of wine." If desired, top the pasta with Parmesan cheese and basil leaves.

PASTA ITALIANA

NOTE:

Cooking tips from Lou: "Numero Uno: Always open a bottle of Italian wine before you start to cook! Once that has been established everything goes better and better . . . just like life in Italy. Think Sophia Loren!

"You must never cook anything without olive oil, garlic, and tomatoes. They work in any combination, in any recipe: soups, salad, pasta, etc. Have another sip of wine! Herbs such as basil (my personal favorite), oregano, fennel, bay leaves, parsley, and pepperoncini all work in the dance of Italian food.

"Think summer: Grow it, pick it off the vine, dice it, smash it, smell it. Ummm! Have another glass of wine and start to cook. See? I told you you'd feel better about life!"

Jade Lasagna
JADE STARLING OF PRETTY POISON

When Jade Starling gave me this recipe, I was amazed at all of the delicious ingredients it had. Then I came to the part about not cooking the lasagna noodles. My first thought was *This has never worked when I've tried it. But if Jade says it works, I will give it a go.* Guess what? Jade is right on target with this meaty lasagna, and the noodles ended up cooking perfectly to just the right consistency. Right on, Jade!

YIELD:
SERVES 10 TO 12 PEOPLE

INGREDIENTS

MEAT SAUCE:
2 tablespoons olive oil

⅓ lb ground beef

⅓ lb ground veal

⅓ lb ground pork

1 teaspoon salt

½ teaspoon freshly ground black pepper

2 cups finely chopped onion

½ cup finely chopped celery

½ cup finely chopped carrot

2 tablespoons chopped garlic

2 cans (28 oz each) diced tomatoes

1 can (6 oz) tomato paste

4 cups beef stock or water

2 sprigs (1 tablespoon) fresh thyme

2 bay leaves

2 teaspoons dried or fresh oregano

2 teaspoons dried or fresh basil

½ teaspoon crushed red pepper flakes

¼ cup grated Parmigiano-Reggiano cheese

CHEESE LAYER:
2 cups fresh ricotta cheese

8 oz grated provolone cheese

8 oz grated mozzarella cheese

8 oz grated Romano cheese

1 egg

¼ cup milk

1 tablespoon chiffonade of fresh basil

1 tablespoon chopped garlic

½ teaspoon salt

½ teaspoon freshly ground black pepper

PASTA LAYER:
1 cup grated Parmigiano-Reggiano cheese

1 package of dried lasagna noodles

In a large pan, add olive oil, all three meats, salt, and pepper. Brown the meat, then add the onion, celery, and carrot. Cook for five minutes. Add garlic and diced tomatoes. Cook for 3 minutes. Add tomato paste and beef stock, and stir together. Add thyme, bay leaves, oregano, basil, and red pepper flakes. Bring the liquid to a boil, reduce the heat to medium, and simmer for about 2 hours, stirring occasionally. During the last 30 minutes of cooking, stir in the cheese. Remove from heat.

Preheat oven to 350°F. In a mixing bowl, combine all ingredients for the cheese layer.

Jade says, "To assemble, spread 2½ cups of the meat sauce on the bottom of a deep dish lasagna pan. Sprinkle ¼ cup grated Parmigiano-Reggiano cheese over the sauce. Cover with a quarter of the dried and uncooked noodles. Spread a quarter of the cheese filling evenly over the noodles. Repeat the above process with the remaining ingredients, topping the lasagna with the remaining sauce. Place in the oven and bake until bubbly and golden, about 45 minutes to 1 hour. Remove from the oven and cool for 10 minutes before serving. Slice and serve."

Asian Fusion Garlic Noodles
SHAWN STOCKMAN OF BOYZ II MEN

This is a deceptively simple recipe, but these noodles pack a multilayered punch. Your garlic-loving taste buds are in for a ride! This excellent side dish goes great with grilled fish, shrimp, scallops, chicken, or whatever else you like. Bold choice, Shawn!

YIELD:

4 SERVINGS AS A MAIN COURSE OR 8 SERVINGS AS A SIDE DISH.

INGREDIENTS
Water, to boil noodles
1 lb linguini, spaghetti, or rice noodles
2 tablespoons olive oil
8 to 10 cloves minced garlic
1 stick (4 oz or 8 tablespoons) butter
2 tablespoons garlic powder
2 teaspoons chicken bouillon powder, dissolved in ⅛ cup of boiling water*
2 tablespoons Chinese oyster sauce
½ cup grated Parmesan cheese
GARNISH:
Chopped scallions

DIRECTIONS

Boil the water, then add the noodles. In a small frying pan, add olive oil over medium heat. Add the garlic and sauté until it starts to brown. Turn the heat off, and add the butter to the hot pan to melt it. Add the garlic powder, chicken bouillon liquid, and oyster sauce, and mix together.

When the noodles are done cooking, drain and return them to the pot they were boiled in. Pour the buttery garlic-flavored sauce on top of the noodles. Add Parmesan cheese, and toss together.

Garnish with chopped scallions. Serve immediately.

* Or 1 teaspoon concentrated chicken bouillon (or 2 chicken bouillon cubes) dissolved in ⅛ cup boiling water

All Purpose Spaghetti & Pizza Sauce
Jimmy Greenspoon of Three Dog Night

Jimmy explains, "Put this sauce on your favorite cooked pasta, and it is absolutely wonderful. It also has all of the ingredients for a perfect pizza topping. I had no bread in the house the other day, so I just put this sauce on flour tortillas, rolled them up, and had little Italian enchiladas. You could put mozzarella cheese on it, and make them Italian burritos. You can use this sauce on so many things; it's like using the leftover turkey after Thanksgiving!"

INGREDIENTS

YIELD:
SERVES 6 TO 8 HUNGRY PEOPLE

SPAGHETTI SAUCE:

⅛ to ¼ cup olive oil

½ red or yellow onion, chopped

3 tablespoons fresh minced garlic

8 oz sliced mushrooms

1 tablespoon ground oregano

1 tablespoon basil

1 teaspoon tarragon

¼ teaspoon salt

¼ teaspoon pepper

1 lb ground sirloin steak

1 lb ground mild Italian sausage, casings removed

½ lb ground veal

1 jar (45 oz) Prego spaghetti sauce*

1 can (6 oz) tomato paste

1 can (10.5 oz) tomato soup

1 tablespoon sugar

PASTA:

Water, to boil the pasta

1 to 2 lb pasta

Directions

In a small frying pan, coat the bottom with olive oil and lightly sauté the onion and garlic. When the onions start to get tender, add the mushrooms and continue to sauté. Before you are done, add dried spices, salt, and pepper. Stir, and set aside. "Lightly sautéing the dried spices brings out the flavor in them," Jimmy says.

In a large skillet, lightly brown the sirloin steak, Italian sausage, and veal. When it is browned, drain the fat using a colander. In a large pot, add the spaghetti sauce, tomato paste, tomato soup, sugar, and the cooked meat. According to Jimmy, the sugar "takes the acidity of the tomatoes down and balances them out."

Add the sautéed onions and garlic, and stir the ingredients together. Bring the sauce up to a boil, and turn down to a low temperature to simmer. Continue simmering for 2 hours, stirring occasionally. "If the sauce it is too thick, you can add ¼ cup water," says Jimmy. "Some people like it really thick. I do, but if it is too thick for you, you can always make it a little thinner." After 2 hours it should be at the perfect consistency, and ready to serve.

Boil the water, and finally cook the pasta. Serve the sauce over cooked pasta.

* Jimmy says, "I know it sounds bizarre putting a large jar of premade Prego spaghetti sauce in this, but I prefer Prego because it has something in it that I really like. The other stuff tastes like crap." If you want to opt out of premade spaghetti sauce, use 3 cans (15 oz each) of tomato sauce, plus one extra tablespoon of oregano. Suggestion: top with Parmesan cheese and sliced fresh basil.

"Quick and Stiff" Spinach Lasagna
Cherry Vanilla

According to Cherry, "The thing that makes this lasagna so great is that you don't cook the pasta first. You put it into the pan uncooked. It absorbs the liquid while baking! I like to serve it with a simple green salad, garlic bread, a nice glass of Chianti wine, and, voila!"

Ingredients

1 package (16 oz) frozen chopped spinach (or 3 cups freshly chopped spinach)

1 container (15 oz) ricotta cheese

1 whole egg

2 cups grated Parmesan cheese

½ teaspoon salt

½ teaspoon ground black pepper

¼ cup olive oil

5 cups red marinara sauce*

6 to 9 uncooked regular lasagna noodles

1 cup fresh sliced zucchini (optional)

½ cup fresh chopped onions (optional)

¼ cup fresh chopped basil, to garnish (optional)

2 cups shredded mozzarella cheese

3 cups extra red marinara sauce, to serve (optional)

YIELD:
SERVES 4 TO 6 PEOPLE

Let the frozen chopped spinach defrost in a bowl (or use freshly chopped spinach). Preheat oven to 350°F. Mix the spinach, ricotta, whole egg, ½ cup Parmesan cheese, salt, and pepper. Do not remove any liquid from the spinach as it will be absorbed by the noodles.

Add olive oil to the bottom of a 9 x 13-inch rectangular baking pan, spreading it out evenly. Add 1 cup red marinara sauce to the baking pan, and spread it out evenly. Add a layer of 3 or 4 uncooked lasagna noodles side by side, on top of the sauce and olive oil. Top with half of the ricotta and spinach mixture. Cover with ½ cup Parmesan cheese. Optional: if you are adding zucchini, onions, and basil, spread out half of the vegetables on this layer. Cover with 1 cup mozzarella cheese. Add 2 cups red marinara sauce, evenly covering the layer.

Repeat this process: a layer of noodles, a layer of spinach and ricotta, a layer of ½ cup Parmesan cheese, optional vegetables, and a layer of the remaining 1 cup mozzarella cheese. Spread the remaining 2 cups red marinara sauce on top. Sprinkle with the remaining ½ cup Parmesan cheese. Cover the pan with aluminum foil, "tenting" it in the center to avoid sticking, and cook in the oven for 30 minutes. Remove the aluminum foil, and cook for an additional 30 to 40 minutes. Remove from oven, and let it sit for 5 minutes before slicing and serving.

"Make sure it's cooked all the way through. Let it bubble and burn slightly on top of you like it that way (I do!). Serve it with extra marinara sauce (optional)!" says Cherry.

* For an easy Marinara Sauce recipe for this lasagna, see page 134-135.

Ziti & Turkey Meatballs
Freddy Cannon

When I asked Freddy Cannon for his favorite pasta dish, he enthusiastically replied, "Ziti and turkey meatballs!" Take it from the man who first hit the Top Ten in 1959 with "Tallahassee Lassie"–this is an Italian classic! Freddy's advice to me: "Keep on eating!" With this great recipe, it's a pleasure! Suggestion: serve with a fresh green salad.

YIELD:

ENOUGH PASTA FOR 4 PEOPLE

INGREDIENTS

MARINARA SAUCE:

1 cup chopped onion

⅛ cup chopped garlic

1 chopped red bell pepper

¼ cup olive oil

⅛ cup chopped fresh oregano

1 can (28 oz) diced tomatoes

1 can (28 oz) tomato sauce

½ cup red wine

½ teaspoon salt

½ teaspoon ground black pepper

TURKEY MEATBALLS:

2 lb ground turkey

2 eggs

1 cup breadcrumbs

⅓ cup Parmesan cheese

1 tablespoon chopped fresh oregano

1 finely chopped garlic clove

¼ finely chopped onion

1 teaspoon chopped basil

½ teaspoon salt

½ teaspoon pepper

PASTA:

Water, to boil the pasta

1 lb ziti pasta

TOPPINGS (OPTIONAL):

Grated Parmesan cheese

Chopped fresh basil

Put the onion, garlic, and red bell pepper in a large pot with olive oil. Sauté the vegetables over medium heat, and when they begin to tenderize, add fresh oregano. Give it a stir for 1 or 2 minutes, then add the diced tomatoes, tomato sauce, red wine, salt, and pepper. Bring the sauce to a slow boil, then immediately turn it down and simmer for 45 minutes, stirring occasionally until it thickens.

Preheat oven to 350°F. Mix all ingredients together by hand. Form the meatballs into bite-sized balls about the size of ping-pong balls. For uniformity, use a tablespoon to measure the amount of meat mixture in each ball. On a large Pyrex baking pan or cookie sheet, bake the meatballs for 30 minutes.

Put on a pot of water for the ziti, and prepare according to the directions, or until it is done to your liking. Drain the pasta. You are ready to serve: pasta, meatballs, and sauce.

Suggested optional toppings: extra grated Parmesan cheese, and chopped fresh basil.

Manicotti
MARK BEGO

Manicotti is one of my favorite Italian recipes. It is absolutely perfect for a dinner party. You can make it in a large baking pan and serve as is, or use long and narrow individual baking dishes with 2 cheese-filled manicotti per serving.

YIELD:
SERVES 6 TO 7 PEOPLE

INGREDIENTS

Marinara sauce:

1 cup chopped onion

⅛ cup chopped garlic

1 chopped red bell pepper

¼ cup olive oil

⅛ cup chopped fresh oregano

1 can (28 oz) diced tomatoes

1 can (28 oz) tomato sauce

½ cup red wine (Merlot, Cabernet Sauvignon, Chianti, or whatever red wine you like!)

½ teaspoon salt

½ teaspoon ground black pepper

Filling:

15 oz ricotta cheese

1 cup grated Parmesan cheese

8 oz shredded mozzarella cheese

2 cups chopped fresh raw spinach

½ cup chopped fresh basil

2 eggs

1 teaspoon salt

1 teaspoon ground black pepper

½ teaspoon ground nutmeg

Pasta:

Water, to boil the pasta

1 box (14 individual pieces) manicotti shells

Place the onion, garlic, and red bell pepper into a large pot, with the olive oil, and sauté the vegetables over medium heat. When they begin to tenderize, add the fresh oregano and give it a stir for 1 or 2 minutes. Add the diced tomatoes, tomato sauce, red wine, salt, and pepper. Bring the sauce up to a slow boil, then immediately turn it down and simmer for 45 minutes, until it thickens.

in a large mixing bowl, add the ricotta, Parmesan, mozzarella, raw spinach, basil, eggs, salt, pepper, and nutmeg. Mix the filling with a large mixing spoon or with your hands.

Put a very large pot of water on the stove and bring to a full boil. Boil the manicotti shells for 6 to 7 minutes so they soften up but are al dente and still firm enough to handle and stuff with the filling. Remove from the stove, drain, and soak in cold water so you can handle the individual shells.

Preheat the oven to 350°F. In a large baking pan, pour in ½ inch sauce using a ladle. Stuff the shells by hand so you don't break them. As you stuff the 14 shells, place them one by one in the sauce, neatly lining them up without overcrowding them. Finally, ladle more sauce on top to cover the stuffed manicotti. Place the uncovered pan(s) into the oven, and bake for 35 minutes. Let cool for 5 minutes before serving. Carefully serve on individual plates, with extra sauce.

Rigatoni Bolognese
MARK BEGO

If you are looking for a pasta sauce recipe that is bold and meaty, this Bolognese sauce is without a doubt a sheer winner. It is easy to make and packed with flavor, and it really clings to pasta. Traditionally, it is served with rigatoni, but it can also be served on spaghetti, linguini, or whatever happens to be your favorite shape of pasta.

YIELD:

Serves 4 hungry people as a full meal or 6 people with salad and sides

INGREDIENTS
8 slices bacon
1 lb ground beef
1 lb ground veal, pork, or turkey
6 tablespoons olive oil
2 tablespoons butter
1 large chopped onion
2 stalks chopped celery
4 to 6 cloves chopped garlic
1 cup grated or chopped carrots
1 can (28 oz) crushed or whole tomatoes
1 can (15 oz) tomato sauce
2 teaspoons oregano or Italian spice
1 teaspoon salt
½ teaspoon pepper
1 cup red wine (Merlot, Chianti, or Cabernet)
Water, to boil the pasta
1 lb rigatoni, or any other shape of pasta
2 cups grated Parmesan cheese, to garnish
Chopped or whole fresh basil leaves, to garnish (optional)

DIRECTIONS

Brown the bacon in a heated pan, drain the fat, and set aside. Brown the ground meat, drain the fat, and set aside.

Place olive oil and butter in a pan, and sauté the onion, celery, garlic, and carrots. When the vegetables are tender, add canned tomatoes and tomato sauce, breaking any huge chunks of tomato up with your spoon as you stir. Add the oregano, salt, and pepper.

Cut the crisp, cooked bacon into small pieces (kitchen scissors are great for this), and add to the sauce. Add the ground meat and red wine, and stir together. Simmer sauce over low heat for 1½ hours, stirring occasionally. If the sauce becomes too thick at any point, do not add water to it—add more red wine!

Boil a pot of water and cook the pasta. Serve with Parmesan cheese on top. Optional: garnish with fresh basil leaves.

Spaghetti with Tuna Fish
Mark Bego

I was in Paris recently. When it started to rain around lunchtime, I dashed into an Italian restaurant, and there on the menu was spaghetti with a tomato tuna sauce. How bizarre, I thought. The more I thought about it, the more intrigued I became. I had to try it. Much to my delight, it was absolutely delicious! In fact, it was so good that when I got home, I replicated what I had eaten in Paris, taking the flavors up several notches by adding capers, black olives, and a few other ingredients. If you are a seafood lover, you will get into this inexpensive, impressive, and easy-to-make recipe.

Yield:
Serves 3 to 4 people

Ingredients
1 medium to large chopped onion
2 chopped cloves garlic
¼ cup olive oil
¼ cup chopped fresh oregano
1 can (14.5 oz) tomato sauce
1 can (14.5 oz) diced tomatoes
1 small can (2.25 oz) sliced black olives
2 tablespoons capers
½ teaspoon salt
½ teaspoon ground black pepper
1 can (12 oz) white albacore tuna
Water, to boil the pasta
1 lb fettuccini, spaghetti, or pappardelle pasta
Grated Parmesan cheese, to garnish (optional)

Directions

Chop the onion and garlic, and place in a large frying pan or saucepan. Add olive oil and sauté the vegetables until they start to soften. Add the fresh oregano leaves, and sauté for 1 or 2 minutes.

Add the tomato sauce, diced tomatoes, black olives, capers, salt, and pepper. Add the tuna, breaking up the larger tuna chunks.

Bring the sauce to a boil, and simmer. Boil the water for the pasta, and add in the pasta. When the pasta is cooked, drain and serve with generous helping of sauce. Optional: garnish with Parmesan cheese.

NOTE: Some people balk at the idea of using cheese of any sort on fish. However, grated Parmesan cheese can be used on top of this tuna pasta sauce–think of a classic tuna melt sandwich.

Chinese Cold Sesame Noodles

Mark Bego

These easy-to-make noodles are absolutely addicting, especially if you love spicy food! I first had these at a restaurant near my apartment in Greenwich Village, New York, in the 1980s, which I would always frequent with Glenn Hughes of The Village People. It can be served as a main course, an appetizer, or a side course.

Yield:

As a side dish to a Chinese meal, serves 4 people

Ingredients

Water, to boil the noodles

½ lb lo mein noodles (spaghetti or linguini will work as well)

3 tablespoons organic peanut butter*

2 tablespoons sesame oil

2 tablespoons soy sauce

2 tablespoons sweet Asian rice cooking wine

3 tablespoons vegetable broth**

1 tablespoon hoisin sauce

2 to 3 tablespoons Chinese hot chili oil

1 tablespoon whole sesame seeds

Garnish

2 to 3 sliced scallions

Additional sesame seeds (optional)

Directions

Boil a pot of water on the stove. Cook the lo mein noodles, drain, and rinse with cold water. This is a dish you want to serve cold, so don't worry about the noodles cooling off.

Combine the peanut butter, sesame oil, soy sauce, cooking wine, vegetable broth, hoisin sauce, chili oil, and sesame seeds in a small saucepan over low to medium heat, stirring constantly for 3 to 4 minutes, until the mixture is of a uniform consistency.

Cool slightly for 1 or 2 minutes, then pour over the cooked lo mein noodles and toss. Refrigerate for 1 to 2 hours before serving. Garnish with sliced scallions and sesame seeds (optional). Serve cold.

* Do not use commercial processed peanut butter spreads. Instead, get the natural organic peanut butter that separates in the jar. Before using it, stir it up in the jar.
** Dissolve 1 vegetable bouillon cube in 1 cup of hot water to make the broth.

Alternative: Hot Sesame Noodles with Shrimp
I have also served this dish hot with cooked shrimp. With this method, after the noodles are cooked, do not rinse them in cold water, or in any water for that matter—simply drain and keep hot. Toss the noodles with sauce, add cooked shrimp, sprinkle with chopped scallions and sesame seeds, and serve.

POULTRY

If you are looking for new and exciting ways to prepare chicken or turkey, look no further! Michelle Phillips of The Mamas & The Papas has a brilliant and elegant way to prepare it with a fresh citrus twist with her Organic Lemon Chicken (page 154). If you like it spicy, try Boz Scaggs's Tuscan Devil's Chicken (page 146) or Tiffany's exotic Lebanese Cinnamon Chicken (page 152). If you are looking for a more soulful recipe, Martha Reeves' unique Smoked Turkey Necks & Lima Beans (page 148) packs a lot of flavor. And if you are planning a dinner party, Marilyn McCoo shows you how to make her sweet and sour Polynesian Chicken (page 156), which is astonishingly delicious.

Credit: Garrett Miller

Credit: MJB Photo Archives

LEFT: Billy Davis, Jr., the gorgeous Marilyn McCoo, and I were together to celebrate Mary Wilson's birthday in 2016 at Nic's Martini Lounge in Beverly Hills, California.
RIGHT: Whenever I see Martha Reeves, I cannot stop smiling! Here we are in 2014 in Hartford, Connecticut, at a gala benefit where she was the very special "guest of honor" and star of the evening.

Tuscan Devil's Chicken
BOZ SCAGGS

When I had the opportunity to interview Boz Scaggs about his music, I found out that he grows grapes for his own wine and loves to come up with recipes to pair with it. When he sent his three variations on Tuscan grilled chicken to me, I decided to test drive his recipe for Tuscan chicken thighs: *pollo al diavolo* (Italian for "devil's chicken"). This is truly the "lowdown" on how to make chicken thighs "Boz Scaggs" style. Pair it with a nice Chianti or Zinfandel wine.

YIELD:
SERVES 3 TO 4 PEOPLE

INGREDIENTS

1 cup red wine vinegar

½ cup olive oil

4 to 6 boneless chicken thighs

1 tablespoon dried rosemary leaves

1 tablespoon sage

1 tablespoon garlic powder

1 tablespoon sea salt

1 tablespoon dried lemon peel

1 teaspoon ground black pepper

1 teaspoon crushed red pepper flakes

Freshly squeezed lemon juice, to drizzle

Olive oil, to drizzle

1 sliced lemon, to garnish

Combine the red wine vinegar and olive oil in a large bowl or zippered plastic bag. Marinate the chicken thighs in the bag for 1 hour.

Combine the Tuscan herbs—rosemary, sage, garlic powder, sea salt, lemon peel—and black pepper and red pepper flakes. Remove the marinated chicken from the liquid marinade, and rub with the spice rub.

Place the marinated chicken in a pan over medium heat on the stove. Wrap bricks in aluminum foil and place on top of the chicken (you can also use another frying pan as a weight) to press more of the meat into the cooking surface. (You can also simply press the chicken onto the pan with a spatula to achieve this effect.) After 5 to 7 minutes, remove the weights, turn over the chicken, and replace the weights to cook the other side, another 5 to 7 minutes.

Judge the degree of doneness of the chicken by slicing into the middle of one of the pieces to make certain it is cooked thoroughly. When the chicken is done in the middle, plate it. Drizzle with freshly squeezed lemon juice and olive oil. Garnish with lemon slices.

NOTE: You can also find premixed Tuscan herbs (rosemary, sage, garlic powder, sea salt, lemon peel) in grocery stores.

Smoked Turkey Necks & Lima Beans
MARTHA REEVES

"This is *real* soul food!" Martha says. "I made this for Eddie Kendricks before he died, because he asked me to." You know Martha from her unforgettable hits "Jimmy Mack," "Dancing in the Street," and "Honey Chile"; now let me introduce you to Chef Martha! Martha proudly points out, "I am from the South, and this was one of my mother's favorite recipes." I met Martha's mom, Ruby, in the 1990s, and it makes me happy to honor her by sharing this Southern classic.

YIELD:

SERVES 3 TO 4 PEOPLE

INGREDIENTS
1 lb dried lima beans*
2 smoked turkey necks**
1 tablespoon salt
1 tablespoon rosemary
1 tablespoon thyme
1 tablespoon parsley
1 tablespoon sage
1 tablespoon cayenne pepper
4 to 6 cups water
1 chopped onion

* "Go through the beans," says Martha. "You don't want to have any broken or brown beans. You want perfectly whole beans."
** She also advises, "Make sure the smoked turkey necks are nice and meaty, as a little one has no meat to it."

Place the lIma beans, turkey necks, salt, rosemary, thyme, parsley, sage, and cayenne pepper in a pot with 4 cups of water. If there is not enough water, add more, just enough so the ingredients are covered. Bring to a boil for 20 minutes. After 20 minutes, the turkey meat should fall off the bones. Carefully remove the bones and skin from the pot, leaving the meat, spices, and beans.

Next, Chef Martha instructs, "Bones out, onions in." Add the onion to the pot. Bring to a rapid boil, then turn the heat down and simmer at a low temperature, an additional 20 minutes.

At that point, sample the beans to make sure they are cooked. Martha warns, "They should be soft to the taste. Cook them a maximum of 45 minutes. Do not overcook them. You don't want mushy lima beans!"

NOTE: Martha suggests, "Serve this with cornbread or greens." Now that is what I call the ultimate soul food meal!

Mexican Tortilla Chicken Casserole
DEBBY CAMPBELL

Debby Campbell says, "This is a recipe that I used to make for my father." And her father is, in fact, the great Glen Campbell! In a fun twist of irony, this can also be made with Campbell brand canned soups! Like all Mexican-inspired dishes, you can always take the spiciness "to the next level" by adding your favorite hot sauce. This is a great dish for a small dinner party—serve it with a green salad.

YIELD:

SERVES 4 PEOPLE

INGREDIENTS
1 skinless whole chicken or
   4 chicken breasts*
1 cup chicken broth
1 can (10.5 oz) cream of chicken
   soup
1 can (10.5 oz) cream of
   mushroom soup
12 corn tortillas
1½ cups chopped onions
2 cans (4 oz each) Mexican
   green chilies
2 cups grated sharp Cheddar
   cheese
1 to 2 jalapeño peppers,
   chopped (optional)

TOPPINGS:
Hot or mild taco sauce or salsa,
   to garnish (optional)

* You can also use a whole
precooked rotisserie chicken.

Either precook 4 chicken breasts or bake a whole chicken for 1 hour at 350°F in the oven. When the chicken has cooled off enough to handle, remove the flesh from the bone and chop or shred into medium and small pieces.

Mix together the chicken broth, cream of chicken soup, and cream of mushroom soup in a bowl, and set aside. Cut the tortillas into quarters.

Preheat oven to 350°F. In a medium to large baking pan, begin to layer the ingredients as though you were creating a Mexican lasagna. According to Debby, "Begin and end with chicken." Spread one third of the chicken pieces on the bottom of the baking pan, followed by one third of the onions, and one third of the green chilies. Cover the layer with one half of the quartered corn tortillas, arranged on top. Using a large spoon or ladle, cover the chicken and tortilla mixture with one third of the soup and broth mixture, and sprinkle it with one third of the Cheddar cheese.

Spread the second layer of one third of the chicken, one third of the onions, one third of the green chilies, and sprinkle in the jalapeño peppers (optional, if you like it spicy). Evenly cover with a second layer of the remaining half of the tortillas. Top the layer with another third of the soup and broth mixture, followed by another third of Cheddar cheese.

For the third and final layer, spread out the last of the chicken, onions, and green chilies evenly. Top with the rest of the soup and broth mixture, and cover with the last of the Cheddar cheese.

Bake in the oven for 1 hour. Top the individual helpings of casserole with stripes of your favorite taco sauce or salsa.

Lebanese Cinnamon Chicken
TIFFANY

Drawing on her Lebanese, Syrian, Irish, and Cherokee background, Tiffany shows off her deliciously spicy Lebanese recipe, and it's absolutely excellent! The lemon juice, olives, garlic, cinnamon, and exotic spices make this a sheer winner. This chicken recipe is a unique and flavorful change of pace that I highly recommend. Tiffany recommends, "Serve this over cooked couscous or rice." I also tried this over noodles, and the effect was equally wonderful!

YIELD:

SERVES 6 PEOPLE

INGREDIENTS
1 large whole chicken, cut into pieces
¼ cup olive oil
½ teaspoon salt
½ teaspoon ground black pepper
¼ cup chopped fresh garlic
½ cup fresh lemon juice
⅓ cup sliced Kalamata olives
2 medium chopped onions
1 teaspoon ground cinnamon
1 teaspoon paprika
1 teaspoon cayenne pepper
1 teaspoon cumin seeds

GARNISH:
2 to 4 cups cooked rice or couscous (optional)
½ cup coarsely chopped parsley

DIRECTIONS

Preheat oven to 425°F. Place cut pieces of chicken in a large casserole dish.

In a separate bowl add all of the marinade and sauce ingredients: olive oil, salt, pepper, garlic, lemon juice, Kalamata olives, onions, cinnamon, paprika, cayenne pepper, and cumin seeds. According to Tiffany: "If you like a spicier recipe, which I enjoy, simply add 2 teaspoons cayenne pepper and 2 teaspoons ground cinnamon." Stir the ingredients together, and pour over the chicken pieces.

Using a baking dish lid or a sheet of aluminum foil, cover the chicken and bake for 45 minutes. Remove the cover or lid, lower the oven temperature to 375°F, and continue to bake uncovered for 15 more minutes, or until the chicken is golden brown.

Place the chicken on a platter atop cooked rice or couscous, and sprinkle chopped parsley on top.

Organic Lemon Chicken
MICHELLE PHILLIPS OF THE MAMAS & THE PAPAS

"I love to share recipes, and when I do I like to give people recipes that are easy to prepare and aren't too intimidating," says Michelle. "This is something that is really delicious! Although it takes a while to make it, this is a very delicate dish that is worth every bit of effort." Serve with a side vegetable and salad.

YIELD:
SERVES 4 TO 6 PEOPLE

INGREDIENTS
2 lb skinless, boneless de-veined chicken breasts (4 to 6 breasts)

8 to 10 freshly juiced lemons

¼ lb butter

4 cups water

2 cups white rice

½ cup beef bouillon concentrate (or Bovril paste)

½ cup Madeira wine (Portuguese dry wine)

2 cups heavy cream

GARNISH:
½ cup chopped parsley (curly or Italian flat-leaf)

2 to 3 sliced lemons

Place the chicken breasts in a baking dish or plastic zippered bag, cover with lemon juice, and seal. If in a baking dish, cover with plastic wrap. Refrigerate and marinate for 3 to 4 hours.

Preheat the oven to 250°F. After chicken is marinated, in a large frying pan (cast iron is ideal), melt butter over low heat. Add the chicken breasts. According to Michelle, "Slowly drizzle in the lemon marinade, so you end up with a lemon butter sauce."

When bubbling, lower the heat and cook 20 to 30 minutes, so that the chicken is no longer pink in the middle. Remove chicken from the pan, place on a baking pan, and place in oven to keep warm.

Boil water, then add the rice. Cover and simmer at a low temperature for 20 minutes. To the lemon butter in the pan, add beef bouillon concentrate (or Bovril) and Madeira wine. Turn up to medium heat. When bubbling, lower the heat and simmer until reduced to half its volume. Add heavy cream, and simmer again until reduced by half its volume over low heat.

Remove chicken breasts from oven and add to pan, simmering in sauce for 5 minutes, turning once.

When the rice is done, either serve on a large platter or on individual plates. Arrange chicken breasts on the rice, and cover with sauce. Garnish with fresh parsley and sliced lemons.

Aunt Mil's Polynesian Chicken
Marilyn McCoo of The Fifth Dimension

The minute Marilyn McCoo told me about this recipe, I was dying to make it! I love a new twist on Asian food. It has that fabulous sweet and sour flavor and the words "dinner party" written all over it. Serve with rice, and you have a total Polynesian affair. You might even want to serve it in your own backyard, with Tiki torches blazing! According to Marilyn, "This recipe is in memory of my Aunt Mil."

Yield:
Serves 12 people

Ingredients

6 whole and halved chicken breasts

6 chicken legs

6 chicken thighs

4 cans (15 oz each) tropical fruit salad*

1 to 6 cloves diced garlic

6 oz soy sauce

5 cups Chinese sweet and sour sauce (or 4 jars, 10 oz each)

6 cups water

3 cups white or brown rice

Preheat oven to 350°F. Arrange chicken skin side up in a shallow baking pan in a single layer.

Drain the fruit, reserving the syrup. Mix the syrup with garlic and soy sauce, and pour over the chicken. Bake the chicken for 1 hour, basting it frequently. Rearrange chicken if necessary, so the skin browns. Meanwhile, cover the fruit, and place in the refrigerator for later use.

Remove the chicken from the oven, and let cool. Drain the liquid from the pan, which is basically chicken juices and fruit syrup, and pour it into a saucepan. Add the sweet and sour sauce to the syrup mixture, stir together, and simmer for approximately 40 minutes. Pour the thickened sauce over the chicken. When it cools off, cover the chicken and sauce with plastic wrap, and refrigerate for a few hours or overnight. NOTE: I have made this recipe first cooking the chicken in the morning, and then doing the second bake that evening, and it worked out great.

About 1½ hours before serving, preheat oven to 350°F. Uncover the chicken and sauce, and bake for 30 minutes, basting often. After 30 minutes, remove the chicken from the oven. Add the fruit. Return it to the oven for 30 or more minutes, until piping hot.

In the last 30 minutes before serving, boil water, add the rice, turn down to low temperature, and cover and simmer at low heat for 20 minutes (45 minutes, if you use brown rice). Serve the chicken and sauce over cooked white or brown rice.

* When Marilyn and I discussed this dish, we both agreed that canned tropical fruit salad was the ideal fruit combination for this recipe, as it usually contains pineapple, red papaya, and yellow papaya, in pineapple and passion fruit juice. However, you could instead use 2 large cans of pineapple chunks, and 1 large can of Mandarin orange segments.

Chicken Soup
THELMA HOUSTON

I was having coffee with Thelma Houston when the subject of chicken soup came up. I jotted down every ingredient she gave me, but there were no definitive measurements, so I decided to give it a test spin to see what I came up with. Take it from me, this recipe gives it the perfect balance. Well done, Thelma!

YIELD:

SERVES 6 PEOPLE AS A MAIN COURSE OR 8 AS A STARTER

INGREDIENTS
4 to 6 chicken thighs (with skin and bones)
8 cups chicken stock
1 cubed chayote squash*
2 cups cubed rutabagas or turnips
1 cup chopped celery
2 cups cubed sweet potatoes
1 can (15.25 oz) corn
1 cup chopped onions
6 to 8 chopped garlic cloves
5 bay leaves
2 teaspoons garam masala spice
2 teaspoons kosher salt
2 teaspoons ground black pepper

DIRECTIONS

In a very large pot over medium-high heat, add all of the ingredients. Cover and bring to a boil, stirring occasionally to prevent any burning on the bottom. When it begins to boil, turn down to a simmer, and continue cooking for 30 minutes.

After 30 minutes, carefully remove the chicken thighs, one at a time. Remove the skin and bones and discard. Return the thigh meat to the soup and continue simmering.

Simmer at low heat for another 30 minutes. Remove and discard the bay leaves before serving the soup.

* Chayote squash is a wonderful addition to this mix of flavors. It has a large seed inside, which should be removed as if it were an avocado pit. The skin of this squash is edible and can be left on.

NOTE: If you wanted to take it to another level, you could also separately prepare cooked noodles to add to the soup. To serve, place noodles in each serving bowl, and add hot soup on top. Don't leave the cooked noodles in the pot with the soup—they will get mushy.

Chicken Mole Enchilada Casserole
Tanya Tucker

Tanya Tucker is one of the most exciting singers in country and rock music, and her take on Chicken Mole Enchilada Casserole is every bit as awesome as Tanya herself! You can certainly make this classic Mexican dish with mole sauce from a jar as a shortcut; however, the homemade sauce below is outrageously delicious and so easy to make.

Yield:
Serves 4 to 6 people

Ingredients

Enchiladas:

3 to 4 seasoned chicken breasts

¼ cup olive oil

1 slivered red bell pepper

1 slivered green bell pepper

1 large diced or slivered onion

¼ cup olive oil

12 corn tortillas (or un-fried flour tortillas)

16 oz grated Cheddar cheese

8 oz sour cream

1 cup of sliced scallions, to garnish

Mole sauce:

4 tablespoons olive oil

½ cup finely chopped onion

2 tablespoons of finely diced jalapeño pepper

2 tablespoons minced garlic

4 tablespoons unsweetened cocoa powder

2 teaspoons ground cumin

2 tablespoons dried cilantro

2 teaspoons ground cinnamon

½ teaspoon cayenne pepper

1 teaspoon salt

32 oz tomato sauce (4 cans, 8 oz each)

8 oz diced green Hatch chile peppers (2 cans, 4 oz each)

2 tablespoons organic peanut butter (the kind that has only peanuts in it)

Preheat the oven to 350°F. Bake the chicken breasts in the oven for 45 minutes to 1 hour. When they are cooked through, remove and let cool. Keep the oven preheated at 350°F. Slice in half, shred the chicken by hand, and set aside. Add ¼ cup olive oil to a frying pan, and sauté the red pepper, green pepper, and onion.

Put olive oil in a large pot and sauté the onion, jalapeño pepper, and garlic until the vegetables begin to soften. Add in the rest of the mole ingredients. Over medium-high heat, bring the mole sauce to a boil, stirring frequently. Simmer over low heat for 20 minutes. Cover and remove from heat.

In a small frying pan, add another ¼ cup olive oil and lightly pan-fry the corn tortillas, just enough so they are flexible and will roll without cracking.

One at a time, roll the shredded chicken, onions, and peppers in the tortilla. Sprinkle some grated Cheddar cheese over the totillas and arrange in a baking dish. Cover with some mole sauce (reserving some to garnish) and the remaining grated Cheddar cheese. Bake in the oven for 30 to 40 minutes.

Garnish with more mole sauce, sour cream, and scallions.

Chicken Paprikash

Mark Bego

This is a great recipe that I remember growing up with. My grandma Catherine used to make it all of the time. My aunt Alice Lizee reinterpreted it and taught me how to make it perfectly. While it is most identified as being a staple of Hungarian cooking, it is a dish that filtered down through the entire Eastern European region. Although I am Croatian and Italian, and not Hungarian, this favorite dish feels like home to me!

YIELD:
SERVES 4 TO 6 PEOPLE

INGREDIENTS

4 chicken breasts (with or without skin), or 6 chicken thighs
¼ to ½ cup olive oil
1 large onion, sliced into long slivers
1 large red bell pepper, sliced into slivers
1 large yellow bell pepper, sliced into long slivers
1 can (14.5 oz) chicken broth
1 can (14.5 oz) diced tomatoes
1 teaspoon salt
1 teaspoon ground black pepper
1 teaspoon chopped garlic, or garlic powder
1 to 2 tablespoons paprika
1 teaspoon crushed red pepper flakes
½ cup chopped parsley (Italian flat-leaf or curly leaf)

¼ cup water
Water, to boil the noodles
3 tablespoons flour
1 lb wide egg noodles
1 cup sour cream, plus extra to garnish

In a large pot or frying pan (a Dutch oven is ideal), brown the chicken on all sides in olive oil on medium-high heat. Remove from the pot and set aside.

Add the onion and pepper to the chicken-flavored olive oil and sauté. When they begin to soften, add the chicken broth, tomatoes, salt, pepper, garlic, paprika, red pepper flakes, and half of the chopped parsley. Stir the mixture. While the sauce and vegetables heat up, place the chicken back in the pot. Using a spoon or tongs, submerge the chicken in the sauce. Bring the mixture to a boil, and then turn down the heat to medium-low and continue to simmer it for 30 minutes, so the chicken will tenderize.

After 15 minutes, boil a pot of water for the noodles. Add flour to ¼ cup additional water and mix together to remove any lumps. Pour the flour and water mixture into the sauce and chicken, stirring it in. The flour will cook into the sauce and thicken up the liquid into a spicy tomato and paprika gravy.

When the water for the noodles has boiled, add noodles to cook. When the noodles are nearly done, remove the chicken from the pot, and set aside. Stir sour cream into the sauce, then put back the chicken, giving the entire concoction one last stir. Drain the noodles, and serve the chicken and sauce over the noodles on individual plates. Garnish with additional parsley and sour cream.

Spicy Turkey Tacos
Mark Bego

I have been a huge fan of tacos ever since I was a teenager. Although I grew up eating tacos made with ground beef, I recently became hooked on making them with turkey. The ground turkey meat perfectly absorbs the taste of all the spices. These tacos are great with all of the toppings piled on top.

YIELD:

SERVES 4 TO 6 PEOPLE

INGREDIENTS

MEAT FILLING:

3 tablespoons olive oil (or vegetable oil)

1 lb ground turkey (or ground beef, pork, or chicken)

½ cup tomato sauce

½ cup water

1 teaspoon paprika

1 teaspoon salt

½ teaspoon ground black pepper

1 teaspoon chili powder

1 teaspoon ground cumin

½ teaspoon onion powder

½ teaspoon red cayenne pepper

TACO SHELLS:

¼ cup olive oil (or vegetable oil)

12 to 14 uncooked corn tortillas

TOPPINGS:

8 oz sour cream

2 cups shredded Cheddar cheese

1 to 2 cups tomato salsa (or diced fresh tomato)

3 cups shredded iceberg lettuce

1 bottle your favorite hot sauce

ADDITIONAL TOPPINGS (OPTIONAL):

Sliced jalapeño peppers

Avocado slices

In a medium-sized frying pan, add olive oil and ground turkey meat. Over medium-high heat, brown the turkey meat. When the meat is browned, add the tomato sauce, water, and the spice mix—paprika, salt, pepper, chili powder, cumin, onion powder, and cayenne pepper. Simmer the meat and spices together, uncovered, at low heat for 15 to 20 minutes until the mixture thickens up.

In large frying pan, add olive oil over medium-high heat for about 5 minutes. Fry as many corn tortillas in the frying pan as you can without overcrowding them. Using kitchen tongs, turn the tortillas until they start to turn golden brown and crispy on both sides. Using the tongs, mark a center point on the tortilla, and carefully fold or curve the tortilla in half while you continue frying them. Give the folded tortillas an extra 1 or 2 minutes to further brown.

Fill the bottom of the taco shells with 1 tablespoon of the spiced meat mixture, sour cream, Cheddar cheese, salsa (or chopped tomato), lettuce, and your favorite hot sauce. Optional: Top with jalapeño peppers and avocados. Let the flavor fiesta begin!

Indian Chicken Vindaloo

Mark Bego

Like all curry powders, vindaloo spice is a blend of several spices—coriander, cumin seed, garlic, red pepper, black pepper, turmeric, cinnamon, and cloves. You could also use standard curry powder, and adjust the heat with red pepper.

YIELD:

SERVES 4 PEOPLE

INGREDIENTS

Chicken:

3 to 4 boneless, skinless chicken breasts

⅓ cup olive oil

2 cups cauliflower florets, cut in fourths

3 cups chopped onion

⅓ cup olive oil

1 can (14.5 oz) tomato sauce

1 can (14.5 oz) diced tomatoes

1 can (6 oz) tomato paste

½ cup freshly squeezed lime juice

2 tablespoons vinegar

1 tablespoon sugar

½ teaspoon salt

1 teaspoon ground ginger

3 tablespoons vindaloo spice

Rice:

4 cups water

2 cups rice

Condiments on the side (optional):

Naan bread

Mango chutney

Hot or mild Indian lime pickle (or mango pickle, lemon pickle, or mixed pickle)

Cube the raw chicken, and place in a wok or large frying pan with ⅓ cup olive oil over medium-high heat. When the chicken starts to brown, remove and set aside. It will cook even more later in the sauce.

In the wok or frying pan, add the cauliflower, onion, and another ⅓ cup olive oil. Sauté the vegetables over medium-high heat until they start to soften up. Add tomato sauce, diced tomatoes, tomato paste, lime juice, vinegar, sugar, salt, ginger, and vindaloo spice. When the sauce is bubbling, add the cooked chicken and stir into the sauce. Turn down the heat and continue to simmer.

Boil the water in a covered pot, add the rice, cover, and then turn down to a very low simmer. Cook for 20 minutes.

Continue to stir the vindaloo sauce occasionally, and taste to adjust spice content. When the rice has finished cooking, serve the spicy chicken vindaloo over rice. To serve, you can put rice on a serving plate, cover it with sauce, and serve it "family style." Accompany with optional condiments on the side, such as naan bread, mango chutney, and lime pickle.

VEGETABLES & SIDES

With so many people going vegetarian or vegan these days, vegetables aren't just accompaniments anymore; they've proven that they can be the star of the show! Who knew vegetables could be so exciting? Woodstock superstar Melanie demonstrates how to elevate Cheesy Corn on the Cob (page 170) to a fantastic new level, Rita Coolidge shows you how to make Spicy Sautéed Kale & Collard Greens (page 184) quickly and easily, and The Supremes star Mary Wilson goes totally vegan with her Supreme Stir-Fried Vegetable Brown Rice Medley (page 172). If you are looking for a great vegetarian main course rice dish, try British hit-maker Mari Wilson's Tomato & Cashew Nut Risotto (page 176).

Credit: Felipe Echerri

Credit: Derek Storm

LEFT: Rita Coolidge is one of the most sincerely talented and charming rock stars around. Here we are at Nic's Martini Lounge in Beverly Hills, California.
RIGHT: Melanie is someone whose music I have admired since 1970.

Cheesy Corn on the Cob
Melanie

Melanie says, "I realize this is not the most complicated recipe in the world, but it is one of my favorite things to do with fresh corn, especially in the summer, when it is readily available." I am from the Midwest, and every summer my family would have corn on the cob several evenings each week. While the truditional method of enjoying this vegetable is to melt butter on it and add salt and pepper, the masterful Melanie takes traditional corn on the cob to the next level. Who knew that Parmesan cheese and cayenne pepper was the "Brand New Key" to totally spicy and exciting corn? It is absolutely Woodstock-licious!

Yield:
4 ears of corn for 4 people

Ingredients
4 ears fresh corn on the cob
Enough water to submerge corn
½ cup butter
1 cup Parmesan cheese
1 teaspoon cayenne pepper

Directions

Remove the corn husks and corn hair from the corn. Trim off the pointed tips and the stem ends of the ears. Place the ears of corn into a pot or a deep frying pan, and put enough water in it to submerge the ears. Turn up the heat until the water comes to a full rolling boil, and cook the corn for 10 minutes. Remove the ears from the boiling water with a pair of tongs. Although they are not necessary, a pair of corn holders can be inserted into the two ends of the corn ears for easy handling.

There are two ways to proceed. The first way is to butter the corn, then generously coat with Parmesan cheese, and sprinkle with cayenne pepper. The second way is to combine the Parmesan cheese and cayenne pepper, and spread half of this mixture onto a cookie sheet or parchment paper. Note: Do not put the cheese and pepper on wax paper, or you will end up eating melted wax. Roll the first ear of corn in the cheese and pepper combination, and once coated, place on a serving dish or platter. Roll the second ear of corn in the remaining cheese and pepper. Repeat the process with the third and fourth ears of corn. In several seconds, the cheese and pepper combination will melt on the corn, giving it a delicious crust.

Supreme Stir-Fried Vegetable Brown Rice Medley

MARY WILSON OF THE SUPREMES

Here is an easy recipe from Mary Wilson's kitchen, one of her favorite healthy dishes. According to her, "This can be made as a wonderful main course, or it can also be served as a side dish. It is a really great one-dish family meal, with an Asian flair."

YIELD:

SERVES 3 TO 4 PEOPLE

INGREDIENTS

4 cups water
2 cups brown rice
¼ teaspoon salt
4 cups chopped
  vegetables*
1 chopped clove garlic
½ cup chopped onion
¼ cup olive oil, peanut oil,
  or your favorite cooking
  oil
¼ cup soy sauce
¼ cup chopped cilantro

DIRECTIONS

Boil water, and add the rice to cook. Add the salt, reduce heat to low, and allow to simmer, covered, for approximately 45 minutes.

In a frying pan or wok, stir-fry the chopped vegetables, garlic, and onion in cooking oil. Mary warns: "Do not overcook the vegetables. Don't even start them until the rice has been steaming for 35 minutes. You want them still slightly crunchy." Season the vegetables with soy sauce.

Spread the cooked brown rice on a large serving plate or bowl, and arrange the stir-fried vegetables on top. Sprinkle it with cilantro right before serving, as you don't want the leaves to wilt in the heat. Mary says, "When I make this, it's the cilantro that really brings out the flavor! However, chopped Italian broadleaf or regular leafy parsley work with this recipe as well."

* Mary explains, "I most often use a combination of yellow squash, broccoli, carrots, and red and green peppers. However, you can get real creative and add snow peas, water chestnuts, or whatever your favorite vegetables are."

Orange Glazed Sweet Potatoes

Thelma Houston

The first time I met Thelma Houston, we were having breakfast in Hollywood and talking about her fascinating career. The conversation turned to food, and the minute she started describing her recipe for Orange Glazed Sweet Potatoes, I knew it would be a winner! Easy to make, and a show-stopping hit at any meal, this dish's taste of orange perfectly complements the natural sweetness of sweet potatoes.

YIELD:

Serves 4 people, if sweet potato is served in halves

INGREDIENTS
- 2 large sweet potatoes or yams
- 2 tablespoons olive oil (optional)

Glaze:
- 8 tablespoons (1 stick) butter
- 2 tablespoons frozen orange juice concentrate
- 2 tablespoons fresh orange zest
- 2 tablespoons fresh grated ginger
- 1 teaspoon of vanilla extract

DIRECTIONS

Preheat oven to 350°F. Clean and peel the sweet potatoes. According to Thelma, "Split the sweet potatoes in half, making 2 servings out of each of them." You can coat them with olive oil (optional). Wrap the sweet potato halves in aluminum foil to quicken the baking process. Place the potatoes on a baking sheet or in a baking dish, and bake for 90 minutes.

Glaze: In a small saucepan, melt the butter over low heat. When it is liquid, add the orange juice concentrate, orange zest, ginger, and vanilla extract. Stir together for 5 minutes over low heat. Set aside until the potatoes finish baking.

Thelma instructs, "When the sweet potatoes are baked, cut a trench in the middle of each half. Put the glaze in each trench and on top of them."

NOTE: An alternate method of preparing this same dish is to peel the sweet potatoes, cut them into large chunks, place in a baking dish, bake them with a sprinkling of olive oil, and add the glaze to the top, right before serving.

Tomato & Cashew Nut Risotto

Mari Wilson

British songbird Mari Wilson says, "I make this a lot, sometimes adding chicken for those who want it. It's really quick and fills you up! A green salad with avocado goes really well with this, and you can even throw some feta or goat cheese on top if you want to pig out! I usually have this as main course but it's also good to serve as a starter or a side dish, accompanied with a green salad. Especially nice in summer with a glass of chilled rosé."

Yield:

Serves 3 to 4 people

Ingredients

1 medium size chopped onion
2 cloves chopped garlic
1 tablespoon olive oil
2 tablespoons unsalted butter
¾ cup cashew nuts
2 cups arborio rice
1 can (14.5 oz) diced tomatoes
½ teaspoon sea salt
4 cups hot vegetable stock
⅛ cup grated Parmesan cheese
Extra butter, to top

Directions

In a large pan, sauté the onion and garlic in olive oil and butter over medium heat until soft. Add the cashew nuts and keep stirring until they color slightly. Add the uncooked rice and stir until the rice has a slight glaze. Add the tomatoes and sea salt, and turn up the heat.

When the mixture starts to bubble, turn the heat down to a simmer and gradually add the hot stock a little at a time, stirring constantly. Let the rice absorb the stock each time before adding more, about a ladleful at a time. Keep adding and stirring until all the stock is absorbed. Check to see if the rice is cooked—it should be almost soft, but with a little bite to it. According to Mari, "I tend to add water if I run out of the stock until it's cooked. Takes about 15 to 20 minutes or so until all the stock is absorbed, but you still want it very slightly 'wet' with a nice glaze on it."

Mari suggests, "Grate some Parmesan on the top, maybe stir in a little butter, and put the lid on the pan for a couple of minutes to let it go all creamy and yummy."

Sheila's Dressing
MARILYN McGOO OF THE FIFTH DIMENSION

"This recipe is from our dear friend, Sheila," says Marilyn. It is a great and really easy twist on regular baked dressing. Serve it with turkey, beef, chicken, or any main course. If you want to make it totally vegan, simply use vegan cornbread and vegetable bouillon or broth instead of chicken broth. I made this for Thanksgiving dinner, and let me tell you, it is nothing short of amazingly delicious. The flavor dimension of the cornbread and the honey wheat hamburger buns makes this surprisingly different, and it is perfect with turkey gravy.

YIELD:
SERVES 8 TO 10 PEOPLE
AS A SIDE DISH

INGREDIENTS

CORNBREAD AND BUN CRUMBLES:

2 Jiffy cornbread mixes
    (or other brand of
    cornbread mix)
2 eggs
⅔ cup milk
1 package honey wheat
    hamburger buns*

DRESSING:

4 to 5 chopped onions
1 to 2 stalks chopped celery
1 stick (8 tablespoons) butter
2 eggs

2 chicken bouillon cubes or 1 teaspoon chicken
    bouillon concentrate
1 cup hot water, to dissolve bouillon cubes
1 teaspoon ground sage
1 teaspoon poultry seasoning
½ teaspoon salt
½ teaspoon ground black pepper

* If you cannot find honey wheat hamburger buns, use honey wheat bread

Cornbread: Bake cornbread as directed on box, using 2 eggs and ⅔ cup milk. When it is baked, tear apart and crumble cornbread and hamburger buns. Allow to sit out overnight, uncovered.

Dressing: Preheat oven to 400°F. Sauté onions and celery in butter until they become tender and the onions are translucent. Beat the 2 additional eggs. Dissolve the chicken bouillon cubes or chicken bouillon concentrate in hot water.

In a large bowl, combine the cornbread and hamburger bun crumbles with sage, poultry seasoning, salt, pepper, sautéed onions and celery, and all of the butter used to sauté the vegetables. Stir in the 2 beaten eggs and 1 cup dissolved chicken bouillon. According to Marilyn, "The mixture should be very moist and easy to turn mushy."

Spread the mixture in a large baking dish. Bake in the oven for 30 to 35 minutes.

Spinach Sauté
SARAH DASH OF LABELLE

I have known the vivacious and lovely Sarah Dash since the 1970s. She has even come out to Arizona to stay at my house and cook in my kitchen. She is an amazing singer, a delightful friend, and a great cook, too. Here is her inventive and tasty way of preparing spinach. "I love spinach!" Sarah exclaims. You will too, if you do it her way! The butter, garlic and onions are out of this world, and the spicy spark of the cayenne pepper sets off the slightly bitter taste of the spinach perfectly. Sarah darling, you are welcome back in my kitchen any time you like!

YIELD:

SERVES 4 TO 6 PEOPLE

INGREDIENTS
3 tablespoons olive oil
3 tablespoons butter
1 chopped Spanish onion
5 to 6 cloves chopped garlic
1 lb fresh baby spinach*
2 tablespoons water
¼ teaspoon sea salt
¼ teaspoon ground black pepper
¼ teaspoon cayenne pepper

DIRECTIONS

In a very large frying pan, wok, or Dutch oven, add olive oil, butter, chopped onion, and garlic, and sauté. Cook over medium-high heat until the onions and garlic are slightly brown.

Next, add the spinach, water, salt, pepper, and cayenne pepper. Stir upward from the bottom, incorporating the hot oil, onions, and garlic onto the spinach leaves. Very quickly, what once looked like an insurmountable mountain of spinach will wilt to about one-fifth its original size. Sauté the mixture for 3 to 5 minutes, depending on how you like your spinach.

That is all that there is to it, and it is ready to serve!

* Sarah shares a shortcut version of this recipe: "I like to use frozen spinach, because the block of spinach almost instantly defrosts, and it works just as well."

Rösti Hash Brown Potatoes
Angela Bowie

Angela Bowie is one of my dearest friends, and she always cooks like a rock star! The biggest trick with this simple recipe is getting your exact stove setting right so that the potatoes brown, without significantly burning them. It took a couple of tries, but finally I mastered it. Angie, you do know your delicious food! According to Angela: "A great supplement to any meal is rösti: the all-time favorite hash brown!" Perfect for breakfast, or any meal.

YIELD:
4 TO 6 SERVINGS

INGREDIENTS

3 to 6 strips bacon
  (or 3 sausages)*
3 large potatoes
¼ cup olive oil
2 cloves chopped garlic
1 large chopped sweet onion
1 large chopped green bell
  pepper (or yellow or red bell
  pepper, or a combination)

* Says Angie, "Bacon or sausages, depending on what you are eating with the potatoes!"

Grate the potatoes to create approximately 4 cups shredded potatoes. Let sit in a bowl of cold water, or they will turn "rusty." Heat a heavy cast iron or other frying pan. Cut up bacon strips and fry them. When they are crisp, you have the option of mixing them in with the potatoes or putting them on top of the potatoes when you serve them.

Ideally, there will be enough bacon or sausage fat left in the pan to cook the potatoes, but I recommend adding olive oil to prevent sticking. Drain water from the potatoes, combine with garlic, onion, and bell pepper, and place in the hot frying pan. Do not cover the pan, or they will become mushy.

Angie says, "Take 15 minutes for the first side of the potato confection. Do not prod! Walk around! Finish your other dishes . . . do not prod! This was my mistake for years. I'd get so hungry that I'd think I could help the cooking process by prodding the potatoes—well, they don't like it, being prodded, I mean. They probably don't like being eaten either. A potato has a life, right?"

After 15 minutes, turn the potatoes over. I found that flipping them over one-quarter of the circle at a time was easier than the potential mess I would have made trying to turn over the whole circle. Cook the other side for another 15 minutes. According to Angela, "Count another 15 minutes, and do not prod! Do not panic if your rösti is very brown; it's supposed to be! A little blackened is okay. I like it. So I let it get dark brown and then slide it onto a big plate, cut it like a pie, and serve."

NOTE: The perfect pan for making these rösti potatoes is a large cast iron pan. It retains the heat for browning and will not excessively burn the potatoes.

Spicy Sautéed Kale & Collard Greens

Rita Coolidge

I was with Mary Wilson on a celebrity ski trip to Vancouver in the late 1980s when we first met Rita Coolidge. We both felt like we had just made a lifelong friend. Rita is not only a brilliant hit-making singer, but she is also a great cook. When Mary first told me about Rita's quick and delicious way of making kale and collard greens, I knew I had to have this recipe. Most people think of cooked collard greens as limp, over-boiled vegetables that are swimming in liquid, and flavored with bacon. Not these! Rita's way of making them keeps them a vibrant green, full of vitamins, and stuffed with spicy flavor.

YIELD:

Serves 4 to 6 people as a side dish

INGREDIENTS

1 lb collard greens and/or kale greens*

¼ cup olive oil

2 tablespoons warm or hot water

¼ cup freshly squeezed lemon juice

1 bottle your favorite vinegar-based hot sauce

DIRECTIONS

According to Rita: "I simply wash the kale or collards, remove the stems, and chop them into bite-size pieces. In a cast iron skillet, add enough olive oil to coat the bottom, and heat the oil just enough for a drop of water to bubble. Add collards or kale and fold with tongs until coated. Add a little hot water to steam, and cover. I find that hearty greens have enough salt, so none is needed here. Uncover the lid occasionally to fold greens until tender, while still maintaining a good green color. Don't overcook, in order to retain nutritive value. Add lemon juice before serving and a good vinegar-based hot sauce. I like Crystal hot sauce from New Orleans."

* If you have never purchased or cooked collard greens or kale before, you might think that 1 lb greens is an excessive amount as a side dish for 4 to 6 people. While the greens look like a mountain of leafy vegetables to start out with, once you cut away the stems and you steam them, they are going to shrink to one-quarter or less of their original size.

NOTE: If you are vegetarian or vegan, this is the perfect way to serve collard greens and kale, without any bacon. This dish also goes along very well with any of the meat recipes in this cookbook.

Asian Style Green Beans
MARK BEGO

The first place I had these was at a Chinese restaurant near my apartment in Greenwich Village, New York. I have always loved green beans, and they are often made in Chinese restaurants with crumbled pork or simply as a vegetarian dish.

I've created and developed this recipe myself, which I've been making at Thanksgiving for years. It has become a very much in-demand menu item every time that holiday arrives. However, don't wait until Thanksgiving to try these!

YIELD:
SERVES 6 TO 8 PEOPLE
AS A SIDE DISH

INGREDIENTS
1½ lb green string beans
¼ cup fresh ginger
1 onion (yellow, white, or purple onions will all work)
¼ cup olive oil
¼ cup soy sauce
⅛ cup sesame oil
½ teaspoon salt

NOTE: If you wanted to make this more of a Chinese main course, you could add ½ lb shrimp to the beans the last 7 minutes of cooking.

DIRECTIONS

Chop off the stem ends of the green beans–kitchen scissors work well for this task. Remove the skin from the ginger with a paring knife, and slice the ginger into cubes or little matchsticks. Peel and chop two yellow, white, or purple onions into little ¼-inch squares or 1-inch-long rectangles.

In a wok, a covered frying pan, or a Dutch oven, add green beans, ginger, onion, and olive oil and sauté over medium-high heat, stirring consistently to coat with the hot oil. In a few minutes, the green beans will brighten up in color. Keep stirring until the skins of the green beans start to wrinkle a bit, about 20 minutes.

When the green beans start to get tender, pour in the soy sauce, and it will instantly begin to steam. Cover the pan so the vegetables can steam and tenderize, stirring them every few minutes. The beans will start to shrink. After the 30-minute mark, taste the green beans to test tenderness. You do not want the beans to be mushy, but you also don't want them to be too crunchy.

Add sesame oil and salt, and continue to stir the beans. By the 35- or 40-minute mark, the beans should be thoroughly cooked and taste incredible.

Roasted Carrots, Turnips & Beets
Mark Bego

I started making these vegetables a couple of years ago, and I can't get enough of them. They are perfect for a dinner party, a holiday dinner, or as an accompaniment to any meal. You can't make too many of them, and they reheat in the oven perfectly. They are even good as cold leftovers in a roasted vegetable salad. This recipe also works with cubed sweet potatoes, rutabagas, and non-root vegetables like orange squash and Brussels sprouts.

Yield:

Serves 6 to 8 people

as a side dish

Ingredients
4 cups beets

4 cups carrots*

4 cups turnips

1 large onion

¼ to ½ cup olive oil

1 teaspoon salt

1 teaspoon ground black pepper

1 tablespoon powdered garlic

3 tablespoons (dried or fresh) thyme leaves

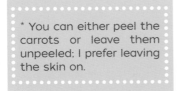

* You can either peel the carrots or leave them unpeeled; I prefer leaving the skin on.

Cut off the long root end from the beets. Keeping the leaves intact, and using the stems as a handle, peel the beets with a potato peeler. Finally, cut the leaf end off. Cut the beets into 1-inch squares or smaller cubes. Roughly chop the carrots in pieces, 1 inch or so in length. The turnips should not be peeled. Trim off the root and stem ends for a fresh clean cut. Cut the turnips into 1-inch cubes. Chop the onion into large pieces, about ½ inch long.

Preheat oven to 350°F. In a large glass, ceramic, or metal baking pan, arrange the beets, turnips, and carrots in strips. Sprinkle the chopped onion over the vegetables in the pan. Pour olive oil evenly onto the vegetables. Sprinkle salt, pepper, powdered garlic, and thyme evenly. Take a tablespoon and give each "strip" a stir, one by one, to distribute the oil, spices, and onions, while keeping the vegetables separate.

Place the uncovered pan in the oven, and bake for 1 hour. Take the bubbling pan out of the oven. Working in strips again, stir the beets, turnips, and carrots separately, to preserve their distinctly different flavors and colors.

Return the pan to the oven, and continue to bake for 1 additional hour. You want crispy edges and melded flavors.

Penne with Artichoke Hearts, Sun-Dried Tomatoes, Shiitake Mushrooms

Mark Bego

In the 1980s in New York City, there was a restaurant on Broadway that had a menu full of really interesting international fusion dishes. I deconstructed this restaurant dish, recreated it, and–in my mind–improved upon it! One of the great things about this recipe is that it tastes just as good the day after you make it. And, it is also great the next day as a cold salad, tossed with more Parmesan cheese. It is "Japan meets Italy on a plate," and the results are fantastic!
Serve with a green salad.

Yield:

Serves 4 hungry people

Ingredients

4 oz fresh shiitake mushrooms or 1 package (1 oz) dried shiitake mushrooms
¼ cup olive oil (if you are using fresh mushrooms)
Water, to boil the pasta
1 lb penne pasta
¼ cup olive oil
1 jar (8 oz) julienned sun-dried tomatoes in olive oil
1 can (14 oz) drained and quartered artichoke hearts

Garnish:

1 or more tablespoons grated Parmesan cheese

Directions

If you are using fresh shiitake mushrooms, cut off the rough pieces of stems, slice the mushrooms, and sauté in ¼ cup olive oil. If you are using dried shiitake mushrooms, place them in a bowl of warm water, allowing them 10 minutes to absorb water. Remove the tough part of the stems and cut the mushroom caps into ¼-inch strips. Return them to the water so that the cut edges can continue to absorb moisture.

Put a large pot of water on the stove and bring to a boil for the pasta. Cook the penne according to the package. Drain the pasta and set aside. In the same pot, add ¼ cup olive oil, sun-dried tomatoes with their packing oil, artichoke hearts, and sautéed fresh mushrooms. If you used dried mushrooms, drain the water and add them to the pot. Gently stir together the vegetables over medium heat. After 2 minutes, add the cooked penne pasta and sauté everything together for 2 minutes.

To plate the pasta, I recommend sprinkling Parmesan cheese on top of each individual serving.

DESSERTS

Everyone loves dessert, and the mind-blowing recipes in this chapter just might make you want to skip dinner and go directly to the sweets! Sarah Dash's Sugar Cookie Peach Cobbler (page 198) is nothing short of awesome. In the mood for cookies instead? Angela Bowie shows you how to make her delicious Cowboy Cookies (page 196), and Tanya Tucker melds together chocolate and peanut butter in her own exciting Chocolate Chip Peanut Butter Chip Cookies (page 206). Looking for something decadent? Thelma Houston doubles your pleasure with her Red Velvet Cake (page 208) and her outrageous coconut-and-pineapple flavored "Better Than Sex" Cake (page 204).

Credit: Charles Moniz

Credit: Mark Bego

LEFT: Here I am, surrounded by beauty: rock & roll legend Angela Bowie and sizzling hot rock diva Sarah Dash, both of whom I have known since the 1970s. We are celebrating Sarah's triumphant 2009 LaBelle reunion tour with Patti LaBelle and Nona Hendryx.

RIGHT: I am partying at the Beverly Hilton Hotel with Tanya Tucker, at the 2017 Academy Awards Night Gala, Night of 100 Stars.

Southern Sweet Potato Pie
MARY WILSON OF THE SUPREMES

"This is one of my favorite recipes," says Mary. "I often make it for Thanksgiving. It has all natural ingredients, and it comes out great every time."

YIELD:
A 9-INCH PIE, CUT INTO
8 SERVINGS

INGREDIENTS

GRAHAM CRACKER CRUST:

1½ cups graham cracker crumbs (from approximately 15 to 20 crackers)

¼ cup brown sugar

¼ teaspoon ground ginger*

8 tablespoons (1 stick) softened butter

SWEET POTATO FILLING:

Water, to boil the potatoes or yams

2 large sweet potatoes or yams

8 tablespoons (1 stick) butter

2 beaten eggs

½ cup brown sugar**

½ cup whipped milk***

⅛ teaspoon nutmeg

⅛ teaspoon cinnamon****

1 teaspoon pure vanilla extract*****

Mary says:
* "I love to add ginger to my crust for extra flavor."
** "Use more brown sugar if you prefer sweeter pie."
*** "Whole, evaporated, skim, or almond milk can be used, as all of these can be whipped."
**** "Cinnamon can be strong so watch the amount, even though it is good for you."
***** "Do not use imitation vanilla flavor."

NOTE: According to Mary, the ingredient list is the full-calorie, excellently rich version of sweet potato pie. However, if you want to cut down on calories or make this vegan-friendly, use almond milk and substitute butter with olive oil or almond oil. Mary also adds, "Other condiments can be used in the filling, like ginger, allspice, and a pinch of salt."

Preheat oven to 350°F. Mash the crackers, brown sugar, and ground ginger until the mixture is well combined. Add the softened butter to moisten it. Pour the mixture into a 9-inch pie pan, and press it onto all sides and bottom to form a uniform shell. Place in the oven for 8 to 10 minutes to ensure that it is firm and browned. Let the crust cool while you make the filling.

Boil the water. Peel the potatoes, cut them into quarters or eighths, place in the pot of boiling water, and cook until soft, about 15 minutes. Drain the water and smash them along with additional butter using a potato masher. Mary suggests, "I like to put it into a blender or food processor to get rid of any strings." Pour the mashed sweet potatoes into a bowl and add beaten eggs, brown sugar, and whipped milk. When it is all mixed together, add the nutmeg, cinnamon, and vanilla extract.

Mary instructs, "Whip it with the whisker to get it very smooth. I cheat and use a food processor." Pour the filling into the baked pie crust, smooth out, and place in the oven for 50 minutes. Let cool before cutting into it, ensuring that it has set.

Cowboy Cookies
Angela Bowie

I don't know what cowboy inspired Angela to concoct these cookies, but these will make you want to instantly join that rodeo! According to Ms. Bowie, "Be prepared for an orgy of taste!" And, you know what? She's right!

YIELD:
APPROXIMATELY 18 LARGE
COOKIES

INGREDIENTS
¼ lb butter
½ cup granulated sugar
1¼ cups flour
½ teaspoon baking soda
½ teaspoon salt
½ cup brown sugar
½ teaspoon baking powder
1 tablespoon evaporated milk
1 teaspoon genuine vanilla extract
1 egg
1 cup crushed pecans or walnuts
1 cup oats
1 cup miniature chocolate chips

OPTIONAL FROSTING:
2 cups powdered sugar
¼ cup whole milk

DIRECTIONS

Preheat oven to 350°F. Cream together the butter and granulated sugar with an electric beater.

Mix together the flour, baking soda, salt, brown sugar, and baking powder, and add the mixed dry ingredients to the butter and sugar. Add the evaporated milk, vanilla extract, egg, and crushed nuts, and continue to blend with an electric mixer. At this point, switch from the electric mixer to a spoon, and add the oats and the mini chocolate chips, mixing them together in the batter.

Using two teaspoons, create a sphere of cookie dough about 1½ inches wide, place on a cookie sheet pan covered in parchment paper, and flatten them out slightly. Make sure you leave 2 inches around every mound, as these are going to rise and spread out as they bake, and you don't want them to stick to each other. I found that making them in batches of no more than 6 at a time yielded the best results.

Bake the cookies for approximately 12 to 14 minutes. As soon as they are golden brown, remove from the oven and let cool before beginning your next batch.

To add optional frosting, mix together powdered sugar and whole milk to create a thick frosting that pours easily. While the cookies are on baker's racks or on waxed paper, line up and drizzle cookies with white frosting, and let them set.

Sugar Cookie Peach Cobbler
Sarah Dash of LaBelle

Sarah: "I don't like my peach cobbler crust to rise much at all. And, I like to sprinkle it with a combination of brown sugar and cinnamon."

Mark: "So, for lack of better words, it is kind of the consistency of a sugar cookie?"

Sarah: "That's it. In fact, you can call it that: 'Sugar Cookie Peach Cobbler!'"

Sarah also says: "I like to serve this topped with either whipped cream or vanilla ice cream. They go perfectly with this cobbler."

YIELD:

SERVES 8 TO 10 PEOPLE

INGREDIENTS

CRUST:

3 cups flour

2 tablespoons sugar

1 stick (8 tablespoons) butter

¼ lb (8 tablespoons) lard

6 tablespoons half-and-half

4 tablespoons evaporated milk

FILLING:

12 cups (frozen or fresh) peaches

4 cups peach nectar or peach juice

6 tablespoons cornstarch

4 cups sugar

1 teaspoon nutmeg

¼ cup chopped dates or raisins

¼ cup chopped walnuts (optional)

TOPPING:

½ cup brown sugar

1 teaspoon cinnamon

1 teaspoon sugar

Combine the flour, sugar, butter, lard, half-and-half, and evaporated milk using either a potato masher or electric beater. Eventually, you will have to get your hands into the mixture and knead the dough until it is of an even consistency. When it is well combined, wrap the dough in plastic wrap and set in the refrigerator for 30 minutes.

Filling: In a large pot on the stove, combine all the filling ingredients. While constantly stirring, bring it up to a boil until the consistency is thick and bubbling, and it is translucent. Preheat oven to 350°F. Pour the filling into a deep baking dish (9 x 13 x 3 inches).

Roll out the dough for the crust, making it large enough for the pan. Cut slits into the dough for steam to escape; you can also cut decorative holes in the crust. I took a small round bottle cap, and, using it like a cookie cutter, I cut stray circles in the dough. Place the dough on the cobbler, and finish the edges by evenly pressing the dough to the sides of the pan by hand.

Topping: Mix the topping ingredients. Sprinkle the brown sugar mix onto the crust. Bake in the oven for 45 minutes.

Honey Yogurt & Fruit Parfait
SPANKY MCFARLANE OF SPANKY & OUR GANG

Although this is a deceptively simple recipe, it yields great results. If you display it right, either in proper raised parfait glasses (like those in the photo) or in tall and clear glasses, this dessert from Spanky McFarlane can be a dramatic hit at a dinner party. According to her, "I can't seem to get enough of this! It is my favorite dessert."

INGREDIENTS

4 cups unflavored Greek yogurt
½ cup honey
½ cup chopped cantaloupe
½ cup chopped fresh seedless watermelon
½ cup chopped kiwi fruit
½ cup chopped peaches
1 sliced star fruit
½ cup raspberries
½ cup blueberries
½ sliced strawberries

OTHER FRUIT:

½ cup sliced seedless green grapes
½ cup fresh pitted cherries
½ cup fresh diced mango
½ cup fresh diced dragon fruit

DIRECTIONS

In a large mixing bowl, add Greek yogurt and honey. Using a spatula or large spoon, fold together until smooth.

Arrange a colorful assortment of fruit in the bottoms of 4 to 6 tall glasses or parfait glasses. When you have a nice 1- or 2-inch layer of fruit, top with a generous helping of yogurt and honey. I've found that placing the honey and yogurt mixture in a sealed large zippered storage bag and snipping off a corner with a pair of scissors creates the perfect "pastry bag" for controlling the mixture in this layering process.

Continue adding layers of fruit and honey-flavored yogurt in an attractive fashion. Finish off the dessert with a mound of yogurt, and top with a slice of star fruit or any other fruit of your choice. Place the finished parfaits in the refrigerator for at least 1 hour before serving.

Hungarian Dessert Crepes
HAVASI

When I asked Hungarian classical pianist and rock star Havasi for authentic recipes from his home country, he gave me these graceful and delicate crepes. Classic!

YIELD:
3 TO 4 CREPES PER BATCH
OF BATTER.

INGREDIENTS

1 cup flour
2 eggs
½ cup milk
½ cup water
⅛ teaspoon salt
⅛ teaspoon sugar
¼ cup vegetable oil

SUGGESTED FILLINGS:

Sliced strawberries
Sliced bananas
Raspberries
Blackberries
Jams or jellies
Whipped cream
Powdered sugar
Vanilla cream
Walnuts
Chocolate sauce

EQUIPMENT:

A large frying pan, crepe pan, or griddle

A "crepe spreader," a special wooden tool to create evenly flat crepes; if you don't have a crepe spreader, use the back of a tablespoon

A long and narrow wooden crepe spatula or frosting spreading knife for turning crepes over without ripping them

Add the flour, eggs, milk, water, salt, and sugar into a mixing bowl, and whisk together. Let the batter sit for 30 minutes. With a heat-proof pastry brush, put some oil a large flat frying pan or a proper crepe pan, and heat to a medium-high temperature. Using a ladle, add batter and quickly and evenly spread it thinly in a circular motion. Ideally, you will be able to spread the batter to cover the entire pan.

Preheat the oven to 200°F. If you have the heat adjusted correctly, it should take no longer than 2 minutes per side. After 1 minute, using a spatula or knife, start to loosen the edge of the crepe from the pan. Don't force it if it is not fully done. Slide the spatula under the middle of the crepe, and in a circular motion loosen the crepe from the pan all the way around. Using the spatula or knife, lift the crepe straight off of the pan so half of the crepe is lifted up in mid-air. Moving sidewise, carefully lower and set half of the crepe onto the pan, and unfold the rest of the crepe, uncooked side down. Cook for 1½ to 2 minutes.

Fill and serve the crepes one by one as you finish making them. You can also accumulate several of them before filling and serving. Place in the oven to keep them warm and prevent them from drying out before serving. Fill them with suggested fillings and roll or fold them into graceful thirds. One very traditionally Hungarian way to serve crepes is to have them with vanilla cream and walnuts inside, and chocolate sauce outside.

"Better Than Sex" Cake
THELMA HOUSTON

When Thelma Houston mentioned that she had a recipe for a dessert called "Better Than Sex' Cake," I instantly wanted it! With a name like that, it had to be incredible. Think of this as an amazing pineapple upside down cake, but with the pineapple on top instead, and a whipped cream and toasted coconut topping on top of that.

YIELD:
1 LARGE SHEET CAKE, WITH
12 TO 16 SERVING SLICES

INGREDIENTS

Cake

3 cups flour

2 cups sugar

4 eggs

1 cup whole milk

3½ teaspoons baking powder

4 teaspoons baking powder

4 teaspoons vanilla extract

1 cup (2 sticks) butter, plus extra
   to grease

Pineapple topping

1 can (20 oz) crushed pineapple

1 cup additional sugar

1 tablespoon cornstarch

**Whipped cream and coconut
topping:**

2 cups shredded coconut

2 cups heavy cream, to whip

1 tablespoon additional sugar

Equipment:

13 x 9 inch rectangle baking pan

Preheat oven to 350°F. Using a handheld or standing mixer, add all of the cake ingredients in a large mixing bowl and blend together until smooth. Grease a 13 x 9 inch rectangle baking pan with butter. Pour the batter into the baking pan. Place in the oven for 40 to 45 minutes. Test cake's doneness by inserting a toothpick into the center–when the toothpick comes out clean, remove from the oven and let cool. Keep the oven at 350°F.

Pineapple Topping: Add to a sauce pan the pineapple (juice and all), sugar, and cornstarch. Over medium-high heat, bring the pineapple mixture to a boil, stirring constantly. When it reaches a boil, continue stirring for 2 to 3 minutes. Remove from heat and allow to cool for 5 minutes. Using a chopstick or a knife, poke holes into the top of the cake to allow the pineapple mixture to drip down into the holes. Ladle or spoon the hot pineapple topping onto the cake. Allow to cool and gel for 1 hour.

Whipped Cream and Coconut Topping: Spread the coconut onto a baking sheet, and toast in the oven for 10 minutes. Whip the heavy cream and sugar. You can either frost the entire cake with whipped cream and toasted coconut, or cut the cake and add the whipped cream and coconut to each serving.

Chocolate Chip Peanut Butter Chip Cookies

Tanya Tucker

Tanya has nonstop energy, and with these cookies, Chef Tanya proves that she is a little bit country and a whole lot of rock & roll. These peanut butter and chocolate cookies are amazingly rich and yummy. Note: These are not "low-calorie" cookies!

Yield:
Approximately 24 cookies

Ingredients
1 cup butter-flavored shortening*
1 cup white granulated sugar
½ cup brown sugar
2 eggs
2 teaspoons vanilla extract
2 cups flour
1 teaspoon salt
1 teaspoon baking soda
1½ cups milk chocolate chips
1½ cups peanut butter chips**
1 cup chopped pecans

* Tanya says, "I like to use Crisco brand butter-flavored shortening." If you have butter on hand, you can simply substitute 1 cup of shortening with 1 cup (2 sticks) salted or unsalted butter.
** You can also substitute the peanut butter chips with white chocolate chips.

Directions

In a large mixing bowl, place the shortening, granulated sugar, brown sugar, eggs, and vanilla extract. Blend together with an electric hand or stationary mixer.

Mix the flour, salt, and baking soda together using a wooden spoon, and add to the batter. Finally add in and mix the milk chocolate chips, peanut butter chips, and chopped pecans. Note: This recipe calls for a large amount of candy chips and nuts and the batter will become very dense, so I usually get my hands into the batter to mix.

Preheat the oven to 375°F. Cover a cookie sheet with parchment paper to avoid burnt cookie bottoms. Using a tablespoon, dig into the chunky batter and form a ball around the size of a golf ball (1½ inches in diameter). Roll the ball in your hands, place on the parchment paper, and flatten slightly. The cookies are going to expand in the oven to around 4 inches in diameter, so I recommend baking these in batches of 6 at a time. Bake for 15 to 18 minutes.

Red Velvet Cake
THELMA HOUSTON

Thelma Houston is a wonderful cook, and every recipe she has given me has turned out great. We had a back-and-forth dialogue about how exactly to make this cake, before we finally agreed that it needed twice as much frosting as either of our original recipes called for. Thelma says, "I really like the slightly crunchy look and taste of the pecans. I would put them on the sides so you have the smooth look of the white on top, pecans on the side, and when you cut into it: *shazam!*"

YIELD:

A 9-INCH TWO-LAYER CAKE,

12 TO 16 SERVING SLICES

INGREDIENTS

CAKE:

Extra oil, to grease

Extra flour, to dust

2½ cups flour

1 teaspoon baking soda

1 teaspoon salt

1 teaspoon baking cocoa

1½ cups sugar

1½ cups vegetable oil

2 eggs

2 bottles (1 oz each) red food coloring

1 teaspoon vanilla extract

1 teaspoon vinegar

1 cup buttermilk

CREAM CHEESE FROSTING:

2 sticks (16 tablespoons total) butter

2 packages (8 oz each) cream cheese

2 packages (16 oz each) powdered sugar

2 teaspoons vanilla extract

DECORATION (OPTIONAL):

12 to 18 pecan halves

NOTE: To replicate the red frosting "kisses" on the cake in the photo, color extra frosting with more red food coloring, add to a zippered food bag, snip off the end, and pipe them onto the side of the cake.

Cake: Heat oven to 350°F. Grease and flour two 9-inch round baking pans. Mix flour, baking soda, salt, and cocoa in medium bowl. Beat sugar and oil in large bowl with an electric mixer on medium-high speed until well blended. To that mixture, add eggs, one at a time, beating well after each addition. Beat in the food coloring, vanilla extract, and vinegar.

Add the flour mixture to the wet mixture, alternating with buttermilk, stirring until smooth after each addition. Pour the batter into prepared pans. Bake 35 minutes, or until a toothpick inserted in the center comes out clean. Cool the cakes for 10 minutes, then carefully remove from the pans. Cool 30 more minutes before frosting them.

Cream cheese frosting: In a large mixing bowl, blend together the butter and cream cheese until thick and smooth. Add the powdered sugar and vanilla extract. It will seem that all the sugar won't incorporate, but keep blending and it eventually will. Frost the top of the bottom layer of cake. Place the second layer on top of the bottom layer, then frost the top and the sides. Optional: Decorate with pecans.

Green Tea Cake
MARK BEGO

With its bright peridot-green color, this is one outrageously cool-looking cake! The drama continues when you cut into it to expose the delicious interior of matcha-flavored and cream cheese frosted layers. Serve with vanilla ice cream.

YIELD:
A LARGE 2-LAYER CAKE,
12 TO 16 SERVING SLICES

INGREDIENTS
CAKE:

2¼ cups flour

1½ cups white sugar

1¾ teaspoons baking powder

4 teaspoons matcha (Japanese green tea powder)

3 eggs

¾ cup butter, softened

¾ cup milk

Extra butter, to grease

CREAM CHEESE FROSTING*:

½ cup (1 stick) butter, room temperature

8 oz cream cheese, room temperature

1 lb powdered sugar

6 teaspoons pure vanilla extract

TOPPING:

2 teaspoons matcha

Preheat the oven to 350°F. In a large mixing bowl, place the flour, sugar, baking powder, and matcha powder. Mix together. Add the eggs, butter, and milk to the dry ingredients, and blend together with an electric mixer for 5 to 7 minutes so that is thick and smooth. Grease two 9-inch nonstick cake pans with butter, and pour half of the batter into each of them. Evenly smooth out the batter in the pan to avoid it from mounding too much in the middle.

Place the pans evenly in the oven and bake at 350°F for 25 to 30 minutes. Since all ovens vary a bit, at 20 minutes, test the cakes by poking the centers with a clean toothpick. If it comes out clean, the cakes are done. Let cool for 3 to 5 minutes. Take the cakes out of the pans. The easiest way is to place parchment paper on a large dinner plate, balance it parchment paper side down on top of the cake pan, and flip the cake out of the pan onto the dinner plate.

Cream cheese frosting: With an electric mixer, blend together the butter and cream cheese in a medium or large mixing bowl. Add the powdered sugar and vanilla extract, and continue blending until fluffy. This recipe gives you enough frosting to evenly cover both layers and the sides of this cake (for ½-inch-thick frosting, simply double the recipe). Frost the top of the bottom layer, and smooth it out. Place the second layer of the cake on the frosted bottom and smoothly frost the top of the second layer and the sides. Using a cake plate with a stem is perfect for you to turn the cake as you evenly smooth out the frosting on the side.

Topping: For the final touch, use a fine-screened hand-held sieve to dust the top of the cake evenly with bright green matcha.

* Double this recipe if you want extra-thick frosting.

French Macarons
MARK BEGO

These colorful, exotic, and mesmerizing cookies are all the rage in the culinary world. Making macarons from scratch is a time consuming and daunting task. It may take you a couple of batches to get it perfectly right. However, when you get the formula right, *ooh la la! C'est fantastique!*

YIELD:
APPROXIMATELY 21 MACARONS

INGREDIENTS

1¾ cups powdered sugar

1 cup almond flour

½ cup egg whites (from 4 large eggs)

¼ teaspoon cream of tartar powder

¼ cup granulated sugar

½ teaspoon any flavoring: extract or oil*

2 to 5 drops liquid or gel food coloring**

Fillings***

Here are six macaron varieties:

* Flavoring:
Blueberry macaron = blueberry flavoring
Orange macaron = orange extract
Passion fruit macaron = passion fruit extract
Key lime macaron = lime oil
Watermelon lemonade macaron = watermelon flavoring
Lavender macaron = lavender oil

** Color suggestions:
Blueberry = blue
Orange = orange (1 drop yellow and 1 drop red, mixed together)
Passion fruit = yellow
Key lime = green
Watermelon lemonade = pink
Lavender = purple (1 drop blue and 1 drop red, mixed together)

*** Fillings:
Blueberry = ½ cup blueberry preserves
Orange = ½ cup orange marmalade
Passion fruit = ½ cup apricot preserves + ½ teaspoon passion fruit extract
Key lime = ½ cup lime curd + 1 to 2 drops green food coloring
Watermelon lemonade = ½ cup lemon curd
Lavender = ½ cup cream cheese frosting
  –8 oz cream cheese, room temperature
  –½ cup (1 stick) butter, room temperature
  –1 lb powdered sugar

Cut a piece of baker's parchment paper that will exactly fit your large flat baking sheet pan. On the back of the paper, use a pencil to trace the size of cookies you would like to make. The tracing on the back of the paper will help you make cookies of uniform size. This is important since you will be matching up tops and bottoms of these cookies. I've discovered that a typical bartending shot glass is the perfect diameter to trace around for perfectly round circles. Place the parchment paper, pencil writing side down, on the baking sheet pan. Affix the four corners of the paper to the pan with a dot of corn syrup, maple syrup, or any sort of edible glue.

In a mixing bowl, add powdered sugar and almond flour, and combine them with a spoon or whisk. In another mixing bowl, add egg whites and the cream of tartar. Beat at high speed for 4 minutes. After four minutes, while continually beating, gradually add granulated sugar, continuing to beat another 1 minute at high speed. Turn the beater down three-quarters of the way on the setting dial and beat for a full 5 minutes. In other words, you are beating these egg whites into total submission for a consistent 10 minutes. At this point, the egg whites should be frothy, silky, and stiff.

Add the powdered sugar and almond flour mixture to the beaten egg whites, and gently fold into the eggs. When the consistency becomes uniform,

add the desired flavoring and food coloring. Fold into the batter until the color is intense and even. These are supposed to be exciting cookies, so make them colorful! Note: "Folding" is done by hand with a spatula. It involves dragging the spatula along the bottom of the bowl and drawing it upward through and into the top layer. Then you turn the bowl 45 degrees and repeat the process, always drawing upward from the bottom. No downward strokes, or you will break the air bubbles in the egg whites. For this recipe, limit yourself to no more than 18 folds, or you will overwork the delicate batter and the cookies will crack on top when they bake. (If you end up with cracked tops, beat the next batch less, and let them dry longer before baking.)

Snip the very end off a 1-gallon resealable food storage or piping bag, and insert and tightly fit a ¼- to ½-inch nozzle. The nozzle is not mandatory, but it ensures uniform piping of batter. Fill the piping bag with batter and seal.

Here is the part that takes the most concentration. On the parchment paper, pipe the batter into same-sized discs evenly spaced and equally sized onto the parchment paper, following the round pencil outline you have drawn. I like my cookies to be 2 inches in diameter. You will need 24 individual cookie halves to yield a batch of 12 finished macarons. Regulate the flow of the batter by squeezing the bag and forcing the batter out of the nozzle in an even flow. Ideally, the consistency of the batter will flow and run just slightly. You should be able to point the nozzle in the middle of your sketched circle, and squeeze it out from a single point so the batter spreads out evenly in every direction.

As you complete each cookie, let up on the pressure in the piping bag and quickly move on to the next cookie. Repeat as evenly and uniformly as possible, continually forming perfectly flat-topped cookies. If you need to even out the cookie shapes, use a butter knife or thin frosting spatula, but be very careful when you touch them in any way before baking. One trick to eliminating bubbles in the batter and to even out the tops is to raise the baking pan up in the air six inches off a surface, and hit it squarely and flatly onto your kitchen counter or table. You can repeat this process up to three times. You will see any large bubbles pop on the surface of the cookies, and the tops will now be flatter and smoother. You must now let the raw cookies sit for at least 1 full hour, or until the tops of the cookies can be gently touched without your fingers sticking.

Preheat the oven to 300°F. Place your oven rack in the upper third of the oven so that the cookie bottoms don't burn. Bake the cookies for 20 minutes. You should see the rounded tops of the cookies successfully breaking away from the base of the cookie, forming the trademark macaron "feet." Make sure they get the full 20 minutes in the oven, or the middles could be damp and stick to the parchment paper.

Remove the cookies from the oven and let cool. Once cooled, the tops and bottoms should peel away easily from the parchment paper. Place the individual cookie halves on a plate or a piece of wax paper.

You are ready to assemble the finished macarons. Match up the most identically sized halves for the top and bottom. You will probably want the cookies with the flattest surfaces as the bottoms and the most attractive and perfectly formed halves as the tops.

Prepare each individual fruit preserve fillings (except the lavender macaron cream cheese filling): Place the fillings in individual bowls, and stir. To make the cream cheese filling for the lavender macarons, use a hand or stationary electric mixer and blend together the cream cheese, butter, and powdered sugar.

Approximately 1 teaspoon of filling should do the trick per cookie. Spread it on the bottom cookie half with a butter knife or frosting spatula, and affix an equal-sized cookie on top. Give it a clockwise twist, so the cookie tops and bottoms will lock onto each other. When you are finished, they should resemble colorful little "hamburgers."

Repeat the process until all of the cookies are complete.

French Fruit Tart with Vanilla Pastry Cream

Mark Bego

I am going to honestly tell you up front: this is one of the most delicate and time-consuming recipes in this book. However, if you take your time and make it right, it is truly the "rock star" of desserts! This makes a dessert that is as dramatically eye-popping as it is delicious!

Yield:
1 tart, 8 serving slices

Ingredients

Tart crust:
1½ cups flour
1 tablespoon sugar
¼ teaspoon salt
8 tablespoons butter
  (1 stick)
4 to 6 tablespoons water
Extra flour, to dust

Vanilla custard:
1¼ cups whole milk
2 teaspoons pure vanilla extract
¼ cup granulated sugar
1 large egg
2 large egg yolks
2 tablespoons cornstarch
2 tablespoons unsalted butter
½ cup heavy whipping cream

Fruit:
1 lb assorted colorful and ripe fruit. Choose from blueberries, raspberries, strawberries, blackberries, kiwi, seedless green grapes, peeled and sliced peaches, star fruit, figs, red currants, pitted cherries, thinly sliced pears, and mandarin orange segments. The more colorful the fruit, the better.

Glaze:
¼ cup apple jelly
1 to 2 tablespoons white wine

Tart crust   In a large mixing bowl, combine the flour, sugar, and salt. Slice the cold stick of butter into small pieces with a knife, and coat with a bit of the flour and sugar mixture. Add the water. Mix the ingredients with an electric beater, food processor, or, my favorite, a potato masher. Keep adding the remaining flour and sugar mixture to the butter mixture as you stir. Finally, get in with your hands and knead the dough until it is of a nice, even consistency. Wrap the dough in plastic wrap or waxed paper, and place in the refrigerator for 30 minutes.

Preheat the oven to 400°F. On a floured surface, using a rolling pin, roll the dough out into a large round sheet. The perfect pan for this recipe is a fluted tart baking dish, with a metal bottom that can be lifted out after baking. Place the sheet of dough into the pan, and work it into the fluted corners. Make sure the dough is not too thin at the fluted edges. Neatly trim the edges of the dough, and place in the freezer for 30 minutes to set. If you have any pastry baking weights, place in the middle of the pastry to prevent the dough from bubbling upward while it bakes. Bake in the oven for 12 to 15 minutes. When the crust is lightly browned, remove from the oven and let cool. Note: Do not freak out if the pastry shell is imperfect or has some droopy side sections! As long as the zig-zagging outer edges are formed nicely, all will be well. The thick vanilla custard is going to cover any flaws in the crust.

Vanilla custard   In a pot, combine the whole milk, vanilla extract, and half of the sugar. In a heat-resistant bowl, combine the egg, the additional two egg yolks, the rest of the sugar, and the cornstarch, and whisk it together. Over medium-high heat, heat the vanilla milk mixture to a boil, stirring constantly. Remove from heat, then slowly pour half of the hot milk into the egg mixture, beating constantly. Return the mixture to the remaining vanilla milk in the pot, and bring the mixture to a boil, stirring constantly. As you stir, the mixture will suddenly stiffen, which means it is boiling. Remove it immediately from the heat and quickly beat in the butter. Let it cool for 5 minutes. When cool, place a piece of plastic wrap over the surface so that it touches the custard and prevents a hard skin from forming on the surface. Place the custard in the refrigerator for 30 minutes.

Take the heavy whipping cream and make stiff whipped cream with a handheld mixer, or whisk very vigorously by hand. Remove the chilled custard from the refrigerator, and whip it to make certain it is smooth. Gently fold the whipped cream into the vanilla custard to create a light but firm pastry cream, which the French call *crème légère* ("light cream"). Spread the pastry cream into the baked pastry crust, and refrigerate for 1 hour.

Remove the tart from the refrigerator. Now it is time to be creative. Rinse, trim, and clean the fruit you are going to use. In any pleasing design you like, add the fruit to the tart in concentric circles, stars, stripes, or whatever strikes your fancy. Whole berries or any sort or variety work perfectly, and sliced kiwis, peaches, nectarines, or pears make nice overlaps.

In a small pot, heat the apple jelly and white wine just enough so that it becomes liquid. Using a basting brush, gently glaze the fruit on the tart. The apple jelly will add sweetness and prevent the fruit from browning or drying out. Refrigerate the tart for one 1 hour. If you are using a tart pan with a removable bottom, you will be able to lift the tart free from the pan to easily serve it without damaging the crust.

Peach Almond Galette
Mark Bego

This is an absolutely amazing recipe for a classic French dessert. Basically, a galette is a pie-like pastry that does not require a pie pan. This recipe is one of my creations—I combined elements from several recipes and gave it my own spin. The use of almond flour in the crust was my idea, and it produces a thin and delicious fruit pie enveloped in marzipan!

YIELD:

1 galette, 8 serving slices

INGREDIENTS

DOUGH:

½ cup almond flour

1 cup flour

¼ cup sugar

½ teaspoon salt

¼ teaspoon cinnamon

½ cup (1 stick) butter, cold

1 tablespoon water

¼ cup extra flour, to flour

1 beaten egg, to wash

¼ cup extra sugar, to dust

PEACH FILLING:

3 cups sliced peaches*

¼ cup sugar

1 tablespoon cornstarch

½ teaspoon lemon zest

2 tablespoons lemon juice

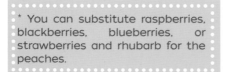

* You can substitute raspberries, blackberries, blueberries, or strawberries and rhubarb for the peaches.

Dough: In a mixing bowl, combine almond flour, regular flour, sugar, salt, and cinnamon. Add the cold butter, cutting it into small bits. Add water. Using a handheld mixer, stationary mixer, or food processor, mix in the butter until it resembles little kernels of dough.

Using your hands, knead the butter into the dry ingredients until it becomes pliable. The heat of your hands will further soften the butter, and soon it will have a consistent texture. Roll the dough into a ball, cover with cellophane wrap, and place in the refrigerator for 1 hour.

Preheat the oven to 375°F. Remove the dough from the refrigerator and remove the plastic wrap. Tear off a large enough piece of parchment paper to roll out the dough onto. Take one teaspoon from the extra ¼ cup flour, spread on the parchment paper, and place the ball of dough on top. Using the palm of your hand, flatten the ball into a thick circle of dough. The dough will undoubtedly crack in places at the edge. Simply patch these cracks with dough to retain a uniform circular shape. Sprinkle another 1 teaspoon flour on top of the dough so the rolling pin does not stick. Coat rolling pin with another 1 teaspoon flour and roll out the dough to form it into a flat piece of uncooked pie crust, about 14 inches in diameter.

Peach filling: In another mixing bowl, add the peach slices, sugar, cornstarch, lemon zest, and lemon juice. With a spoon, combine the ingredients to coat the fruit. Using a slotted spoon, mound the peach mixture in the middle of the rolled-out crust in an 11-inch circle, leaving 3 inches of bare exposed crust around the edge of the circle. Reserve the several tablespoons of leftover fruit juice in the bowl.

Using the parchment paper for guidance and mobility, lift up a corner of the crust and flop it over toward the center, onto a part of the peaches. As the dough sticks to the fruit, carefully peel off the parchment paper, leaving the dough on the fruit filling, thus forming a 1- or 2-inch flap of outer crust covering the fruit. Repeat this process around the pastry in sixths, sevenths, or eighths, until the flaps of overlapping crust form a rudimentary pie crust. In forming this hexagon (six-sided), septagon (seven-sided), or octagon (eight-sided) shape, ensure that the inner 5 or 6 inches of fruit at the center of the pastry is exposed.

Place the unbaked galette, complete with the parchment paper it is on, onto a flat baking sheet. Now, you can pour the leftover fruit juice in the middle of the galette since the crust is folded around and the juice will not leak and burn. I recommend only adding 1 single tablespoon of juice to the center.

Beat 1 egg in a small bowl. Using a basting brush, brush a coating of beaten egg onto the exposed edge of the crust, all around the galette. Sprinkle the additional ¼ cup sugar all over the galette, coating both the crust and the fruit with a dusting.

Bake in oven for 35 to 45 minutes. The desired effect is to have the outer crust nice and brown. After removing the baked galette from the oven, let it cool at least 1 hour so that the fruit juice sets sufficiently and isn't runny.

Boozy Banana Cream Pie
Mark Bego

Banana cream pie is an absolute classic of desserts, and this recipe takes it to a whole new level of deliciousness. Starting with a perfect homemade custard, with fresh bananas and crème de banana liqueur, this recipe takes the banana taste all the way up the excitement scale!

YIELD:
A 9-INCH PIE, 6 TO 8 SERVING SLICES

INGREDIENTS

DOUGH:

1½ cups flour

1 tablepoon sugar

¼ teaspoon salt

8 tablespoons (1 stick) butter

4 to 6 tablespoons water

FILLING:

½ cup sugar

¼ cup cornstarch

⅛ teaspoon salt

1 cup heavy cream

1 cup whole milk

3 beaten egg yolks

3 tablespoons softened butter,
  cut into thirds

2 sliced bananas, firm but ripe

½ cup crème de banana liqueur

WHIPPED CREAM TOPPING:

1½ cups heavy whipping cream

2 tablespoons powdered sugar

2 tablespoons crème de banana
  liqueur

Dough Add the flour, sugar, salt, butter, and water to a mixing bowl. Use an electric mixer or a potato masher to blend the ingredients together. Eventually, you will have to get your hands into the mixture to finish kneading the dough by hand. When it is an even consistency, wrap the dough in plastic wrap, and place in the refrigerator for 30 minutes.

Preheat the oven to 450°F. Roll out the dough with a rolling pin, and fit the crust in a 9-inch pie pan. Place the uncooked pie crust in the freezer to set. If you have "pie weights," place them in the bottom of the crust to prevent it from bubbling. Bake the pie crust for 15 to 20 minutes, and set aside to cool.

Filling In a medium or large saucepan, add the sugar, cornstarch, and salt. Mix together with a wire whisk to prevent the cornstarch from forming lumps. Add the heavy cream, whole milk, and egg yolks. Whisk together with the dry ingredients.

Over medium-high heat, place the pan on the stove, but do not stop stirring the mixture with the wire whisk, or the bottom will burn. Bring the custard ingredients in the pan to a boil. As you are consistently stirring, nothing will seem to happen for several minutes, and then the mixture will suddenly start thickening and bubbling. The second this happens, remove the pan immediately from the heat. Add the butter and keep whisking until it is thoroughly melted and mixed into the custard.

Immediately pour the mixture into a heat-resistant mixing bowl. Take a piece of cellophane plastic wrap and press it down onto the surface of the custard to prevent it from forming an undesirable skin on the top. Cool the custard by placing in the refrigerator for 20 minutes.

Evenly cover the bottom and sides of the prebaked pie shell with banana slices. Remove the cooled custard from the refrigerator, and peel off the cellophane wrap. Pour crème de banana liqueur into the custard in the mixing bowl and immediately whisk together. Pour the banana-flavored custard into the pie shell on top of the sliced bananas. Using the back of a spoon or a spatula, smooth out the surface of the custard, coating the bananas, and creating an evenly-filled pie crust. Place the pie in the refrigerator for 30 to 45 minutes for the filling to set.

Whipped cream topping In a cold mixing bowl, add heavy whipping cream. Using an electric hand mixer or standard upright mixer, whip the cream until it forms stiff peaks. Add powdered sugar and crème de banana liqueur. Whip it all together for 1 minute until mixed.

Remove the pie from the refrigerator and spread the banana-flavored whipped cream on the top. Using even strokes, get creative and make it pretty! Place the pie in the refrigerator and cool for at least 2 hours.

Cocktails

When you are a rock star, any hour can be "cocktail hour." At your next party, you, too, can create delicious, colorful, and dramatic drinks to dazzle your guests. Have a Mint Julep (page 234) with Richie Sambora, a Micky "D" (page 226) with Micky Dolenz, or a Passionate Bourbon Cocktail (page 228) with Mary Wilson. If you want a "vodka-licous" walk on the wild side, Paul Antonelli's Ultimate Dirty Martini (page 232), with its bleu cheese-stuffed olives, is a sheer smash. Let's get this party started!

Credit: Derek Storm

Credit: MJB Photo Archives

LEFT: Micky Dolenz of The Monkees, me, and Mary Wilson of The Supremes celebrate the publication of my biography, *Billy Joel*, in 2007 at The Cutting Room in New York City.
RIGHT: There is literally no party weekend better than the Kentucky Derby, with its clothes, hats, horses, parties, and cocktails! I am enjoying Mint juleps with rock guitar legend Orianthi and Richie Sambora of Bon Jovi fame.

The Micky "D" Cocktail
MICKY DOLENZ OF THE MONKEES

I have known Micky Dolenz since the 1990s when I was the co-author for his hit memoir, *I'm a Believer*. Everyone knows Micky for his rock & roll stardom as one of The Monkees, but many people don't realize that he has also appeared in several theatrical productions on Broadway and the West End in London. Performing solo, he has had a couple of engagements at the cabaret club 54 Below, downstairs from the famed Studio 54, where he recorded an album, featuring not only The Monkees hits, but Broadway hits, too. These engagements were enhanced by the nightclub serving The Micky "D" cocktail.

INGREDIENTS

2 slices fresh orange

4 oz vodka*

1 oz elderflower liqueur
   (such as St. Germaine)

* Micky's favorite vodka for this drink is Tito's Handmade vodka.

DIRECTIONS

Place one of the orange slices in a cocktail shaker, and muddle it (mash, peel, and all with a wooden "muddler" or the end of the handle of a wooden spoon). Add ice to a "rocks" glass. Pour the vodka and elderflower liqueur into the shaker, and shake. Strain and pour into iced "rocks" glass.

According to Micky, "Pour contents over ice, and enjoy!" Garnish the glass with an extra orange slice.

Bourbon Passion Cocktail
MARY WILSON OF THE SUPREMES

Mary Wilson and I were chatting over the phone, updating each other about our latest news. In the middle of the conversation, she said, "I just had the best cocktail. It would be great for the cookbook." That was all it took. I jotted down the contents and was ready to mix up a batch immediately. I have traveled with Mary to some amazing places around the globe. A couple of times, I visited Stockholm, Sweden, to meet her whenever she was performing there. It was in Stockholm that we first adopted our favorite Swedish drinking custom. When two people are to toast each other, they look each other directly in the eyes and toast an enthusiastic, "*Skol!*" We have been doing that with each other for years. This Bourbon Passion Cocktail may not be a Swedish drink, but it will make you want raise your glass with an enthusiastic "*Skol!*"

INGREDIENTS
2 oz bourbon
2 oz passion fruit nectar
  or passion fruit cocktail
2 oz sweet and sour lemon
  bar mix
Lemon slice

DIRECTIONS

Pour the bourbon, passion fruit nectar or passion fruit cocktail, and sweet and sour lemon bar mix into a shaker with ice. Vigorously shake, and strain into a martini glass. Garnish glass with lemon slice.

Lilikoi Lemon Drop
August Darnell of Kid Creole & The Coconuts

It was great to catch up with the multitalented August Darnell recently. We had the chance to reminisce about our friendship, which goes back to the disco days in New York City. We spoke about his Off-Broadway musical, *Cherchez La Femme*, and how August and his lady, Eva Tudor-Jones, split their time between Sweden and Hawaii. I was fascinated to find out that August and Eva have a cocktail lounge, Ambrosia Martini Lounge, on the island of Maui. "I have to have one of your cocktail recipes," I said. Eva contacted me soon after with a recipe for one of their most popular drinks. She says, "This is our signature martini. We named it 'Lilikoi Lemon Drop,' since *lilikoi* means 'passion fruit' in Hawaiian."

INGREDIENTS

1 lemon, one quarter wedge and one sliced wheel

2 teaspoons sugar, to rim the glass

3 oz passion fruit vodka*

½ oz simple syrup**

1 oz sweet and sour lemon bar mix

DIRECTIONS

Slice a lemon and run the exposed flesh across the rim of a chilled martini glass. Pour sugar onto a small plate, and run the rim of the glass through the sugar. Set aside.

Add the quartered lemon wedge to a cocktail shaker. Muddle it (crush, peel, and all) with a wooden muddler or the end of the handle of a wooden spoon. Add 3 or 4 ice cubes, and pour in the vodka, syrup, and sweet and sour lemon bar mix. Shake vigorously, and strain into the sugar-rimmed martini glass.

Garnish the glass with a wheel-like slice of lemon.

* August's favorite brand is Skyy
** To make simple syrup, mix 2 cups sugar and 2 cups water in a saucepan over medium-high heat. Bring to a boil, stirring constantly. Remove from heat, and cool down.

The Ultimate Dirty Martini
Paul Antonelli of Animotion

I have been friends with Paul Antonelli for several years, and I can honestly say that I have never seen him in a bad or depressed mood. A possible reason for this is because his favorite cocktail is the Dirty Martini. As far as I am concerned, these are glasses of instant happiness! And the way he likes to have them is perfectly unique. Paul says, "Oh, my Dirty Martini! I know what you *must* add for the Dirty Martini recipe: bleu cheese-stuffed olives! They must be freshly stuffed with a great quality bleu cheese, such as a Roquefort." Paul and I are such great cocktailing friends that he even calls me "Dirty Martini." Paul, my "dirty martini" buddy, you rock, and so does this cocktail!

Ingredients

3 large stuffed green olives from a jar (stuffed with pimento, garlic, or anything else)
1 block or container crumbled bleu cheese
4 oz vodka*
½ oz olive juice

Directions

Open a jar of stuffed green olives. Remove whatever is stuffed in the olives with a toothpick or thin knife. Using a small spoon or knife, carefully fill the hole in the olive with fresh bleu cheese. With a cocktail skewer, stab two or three stuffed olives and slide them up the skewer, until the top one fits the inner rim of the martini glass you are about to use.

In a cocktail shaker, place 3 or 4 ice cubes. Pour vodka and olive brine from the jar in the shaker. Using olive juice instead of the standard martini addition of vermouth is what makes a "dirty martini" dirty. Strain into a martini glass, and prepare to enjoy the best vodka martini around.

* You can also use your favorite gin if preferred.

Mint Julep
RICHIE SAMBORA OF BON JOVI

Whenever Mary Wilson and I attend the Kentucky Derby and the Barnstable-Brown Gala in Louisville, one of our favorite cocktail buddies is Richie Sambora of Bon Jovi fame. He is always in a fun mood, and he and his entourage of friends are always great to hang out with. When I first asked him for a food recipe, he confessed to me, "I don't really cook much." I thought for a moment and said, "Well, then, how about a cocktail recipe?" While we were busy betting horses, what else were we drinking together at Churchill Downs but Mint Juleps, naturally! So, here from Richie is the classic Mint Julep.

INGREDIENTS
1 sprig fresh mint
2 oz bourbon whiskey
2 oz simple syrup*
4 oz water (or club soda)

DIRECTIONS
Insert fresh mint into a medium-tall glass, and lightly muddle the bottom half of the stem and leaves in the inner glass with a wooden muddler or the back of a wooden spoon. Add ice to the glass.

Add the bourbon whiskey, simple syrup, and water to a cocktail shaker, and stir together. Pour the mixture over the ice cubes and mint in the glass.

* To make simple syrup, mix 2 cups sugar and 2 cups water in a saucepan over medium-high heat. Bring to a boil, stirring constantly. Remove from heat, and cool down.

The Hollywood Cocktail
RANDY JONES OF THE VILLAGE PEOPLE

When I phoned Randy Jones to ask him for a favorite cocktail, he presented me with this incredible libation without hesitation. "This was the official drink of the Brown Derby restaurant in Hollywood," Randy explained. "Pour the Chambord into the glass first; that is the signature way to make these." The Brown Derby was one of the most iconic restaurants in all of Hollywood during its golden era. Part of the original restaurant was actually shaped like the gentleman's hat, the brown derby. Although the actual restaurant no longer exists, this delicious cocktail certainly keeps its memory alive.

INGREDIENTS

1 oz Chambord

2 oz vodka

4 to 6 oz pineapple juice

1 maraschino cherry, to garnish (optional)

DIRECTIONS

Pour the distinctively red and raspberry-flavored Chambord liqueur into a martini glass. In an iced shaker, shake together the vodka and pineapple juice, and strain into the glass over the Chambord.

Optional: Garnish with a maraschino cherry on a skewer or toothpick.

White Sangria
MARK BEGO

Every time I make this recipe, it is a total hit. This perfectly rock-&-roll worthy white sangria tastes like a delicious fruit punch, but with the brandy and triple sec, it packs a delicious "punch"! There are many ways to make white sangria and different fruits you can use, but lemons, limes, and oranges are a must. This exact recipe yields an absolutely perfect blend of flavors.

YIELD:

1 GALLON

INGREDIENTS
1 sliced lemon
1 sliced lime
1 sliced orange
1 fresh skinned and diced mango (or peach or nectarine)
1 pint fresh raspberries (or strawberries)
⅓ cup sugar
⅓ cup triple sec
½ cup brandy
2 bottles white wine (Chardonnay, Pinot Grigio, or any combination of 2 bottles)

DIRECTIONS
Add the fruit in a large pitcher. Add the sugar, triple sec, brandy, and white wine. Stir to mix.

Place in the refrigerator for at least 1 or 2 hours for the flavors to blend. When it is time to serve the sangria, stir it again, and place a colorful mixture of marinated fruit pieces into individual wine glasses. Pour the chilled sangria over the fruit, and serve.

The Sidecar
MARK BEGO

If you were to list the best and most popular cocktails of the 1920s, the sidecar would have to be number one. These are without a doubt the most delicious and potent of all cocktails. Historically, they date back to 1922 at the Ritz Hotel in Paris. I have never had a sidecar I didn't like! I have had them at Joe Allen's and the Waldorf Astoria in Manhattan, and I have had them at the Club Congress in Tucson, Arizona. When made right, there is nothing like them.

INGREDIENTS

- 1 lemon, one lemon wedge or lemon peel curlicue*
- 3 tablespoons sugar (for a sugared rim on the glass)
- 2 oz Cognac
- 2 oz triple sec (or Cointreau)
- 2 oz sweet and sour lemon bar mix

DIRECTIONS

Slice 1 lemon and run the exposed flesh across the rim of a chilled martini glass. Pour sugar onto a small plate, and run the rim of the glass through the sugar. Set aside.

Place 3 or 4 ice cubes into a cocktail shaker. Pour the Cognac, triple sec (or Cointreau), and sweet and sour lemon bar mix into the shaker. Vigorously shake. Strain into the sugar-rimmed martini glass. Garnish with a lemon wedge on the rim or with a lemon peel curlicue.

* To make a lemon peel curlicue, carefully cut a slice of lemon with a sharp knife, and cut away the interior fruit. Wrap the lemon peel tightly around a bamboo skewer, chopstick, or ice pick. Pull the rod away from the peel, and use the curled peel as a garnish either in the glass or on the rim.

Around the World in Cocktails
Mark Bego

Blue Hawaiian

Who can resist a blue cocktail? No one I know! Originally served at the Hilton Hawaiian Village Hotel in Waikiki, Hawaii, in 1957, this drink is a perfect one to serve at a tropical-themed dinner party, or while watching Elvis Presley in his 1961 film *Blue Hawaii*.

INGREDIENTS

1 oz rum

1 oz vodka

½ oz Blue Curaçao

2 to 3 oz sweet and sour lemon bar mix

2 to 3 oz pineapple juice

Orange slice (optional)

Maraschino cherry (optional)

DIRECTIONS

In a tall iced glass, add rum, vodka, and Blue Curaçao. Fill half of the glass with sweet and sour lemon bar mix and the other half with pineapple juice. Insert a straw. Optional: Garnish with an orange slice or maraschino cherry, and top with a cocktail umbrella.

Tuscan Sunset

When an Italian restaurant in Tucson needed a signature cocktail to honor Italy's Tuscany area and cuisine, I invented this colorful and delicious drink.

INGREDIENTS

1 oz flavored citrus vodka
1 oz flavored vanilla vodka
3 oz orange juice
1 oz crème de almond

DIRECTIONS

In a shaker with ice, vigorously shake the 2 vodkas and orange juice, and strain into a martini glass. Pour the bright red crème de almond down the interior side of the glass for a "sunset" effect.

Moscow Mule

This is without a doubt one of the most refreshing vodka cocktails you can make. With vodka, sharp and spicy ginger beer, and the tangy taste of lime, this is the kind of drink you can sip all night long! This rocking cocktail was first served at the Chatham Hotel in New York City in 1941.

INGREDIENTS

1 oz freshly squeezed lime juice
2 oz vodka
4 to 6 oz ginger beer
Fresh lime slice (optional)

DIRECTIONS

The traditional way to drink this is in a copper mug, as it retains the cold and looks so perfectly atmospheric. Add the lime juice, vodka, ginger beer, and optional lemon slice garnish. A light stir will do for this drink, as you don't want to break the "fizz" of the ginger beer.

Mai Tai

The Mai Tai conjures up visions of the tropics, for very good reason, as it originally came from a Californian tropical restaurant. Trader Vic's claims to have invented it in 1944, while its rival restaurant, The Beachcomber, claims they have had it on their menu since 1933. Whichever tropical tale is true, this Hawaiian Punch of a cocktail spells "instant fun" at parties!

INGREDIENTS

1 oz white rum
½ oz triple sec
¼ cup sweet and sour lemon
   bar mix
¼ cup pineapple juice
½ oz crème de almond
½ oz dark rum
 Maraschino cherry (optional)
 Orange slice (optional)

DIRECTIONS

In a tall iced glass, pour in the white rum, followed by the triple sec. Fill up half the glass with sweet and sour lemon bar mix, and follow it with pineapple juice. Pour the crème de almond down the interior side of the glass, so that it sinks down to the bottom of the glass. Pour a "floater" of dark rum on top. Serve with a straw and garnish with a cherry or orange slice (optional) and a cocktail umbrella.

Rainbow of Cocktails
Mark Bego

Cosmopolitan

The Cosmopolitan is such a deliciously tart and incredibly tasty cocktail, it is no wonder that several people claim to have invented it in the 1970s. Then, after the 1990s TV show *Sex and the City* glorified "the Cosmo" as the ultimate sophisticated cocktail, it became all the rage in Manhattan, as well as globally.

Ingredients
3 oz vodka
1 oz triple sec (or Cointreau)
1 oz sweetened lime juice
  (Rose's or any other brand)
1 oz cranberry juice cocktail
1 sliced lime wedge, to garnish

Directions
Pour vodka, triple sec, lime juice, and cranberry juice into a cocktail shaker with ice. Shake vigorously, and strain into a martini glass. Garnish with a lime wedge.

Violet Martini

In Europe, and especially France, the flavors of fresh flowers are often used in food. This amazing violet liqueur derives its unique "Purple Haze" of taste from the violet flower.

INGREDIENTS

2 oz violet liqueur

4 oz vodka

1 oz freshly squeezed lemon juice

DIRECTIONS

In a cocktail shaker or small cocktail pitcher, add ice and all the ingredients. Stir, strain, and pour into a martini glass.

Banshee

This incredible cocktail is perfect as a dessert or an after-dinner drink. It tastes like a banana milkshake on steroids. Absolutely delicious!

INGREDIENTS

2 oz half-and-half or heavy cream

2 oz crème de banana

2 oz crème de cacao

DIRECTIONS

Place 3 or 4 ice cubes in a cocktail shaker with a cover. Add all the ingredients, and shake vigorously. Strain into a martini or other cocktail glass.

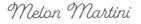

Melon Martini

This melon-flavored green martini has been a favorite of mine for years, and will liven up any cocktail party!

INGREDIENTS

2 oz melon liqueur

2 oz vodka

2 oz sweet and sour lemon bar mix

DIRECTIONS

In a cocktail shaker, add 3 for 4 ice cubes and all the ingredients. Shake vigorously, and strain into a martini glass.

Conversion Charts

METRIC AND IMPERIAL CONVERSIONS

(These conversions are rounded for convenience)

Ingredient	Cups/Tablespoons/ Teaspoons	Ounces	Grams/Milliliters
Butter	1 cup = 16 tablespoons = 2 sticks	8 ounces	230 grams
Cheese, shredded	1 cup	4 ounces	110 grams
Cream cheese	1 tablespoon	0.5 ounce	14.5 grams
Cornstarch	1 tablespoon	0.3 ounce	8 grams
Flour, all-purpose	1 cup/1 tablespoon	4.5 ounces/0.3 ounce	125 grams/8 grams
Flour, whole wheat	1 cup	4 ounces	120 grams
Fruit, dried	1 cup	4 ounces	120 grams
Fruits or veggies, chopped	1 cup	5 to 7 ounces	145 to 200 grams
Fruits or veggies, puréed	1 cup	8.5 ounces	245 grams
Honey, maple syrup, or corn syrup	1 tablespoon	.75 ounce	20 grams
Liquids: cream, milk, water, or juice	1 cup	8 fluid ounces	240 milliliters
Oats	1 cup	5.5 ounces	150 grams
Salt	1 teaspoon	0.2 ounce	6 grams
Spices: cinnamon, cloves, ginger, or nutmeg (ground)	1 teaspoon	0.2 ounce	5 milliliters
Sugar, brown, firmly packed	1 cup	7 ounces	200 grams
Sugar, white	1 cup/1 tablespoon	7 ounces/0.5 ounce	200 grams/12.5 grams
Vanilla extract	1 teaspoon	0.2 ounce	4 grams

OVEN TEMPERATURES

Fahrenheit	Celsius	Gas Mark
225°	110°	¼
250°	120°	½
275°	140°	1
300°	150°	2
325°	160°	3
350°	180°	4
375°	190°	5
400°	200°	6
425°	220°	7
450°	230°	8

Index